1952-1971

Patterns in Pluralism
A Portrait of American Religion

William M. Newman
Peter L. Halvorson

GLENMARY RESEARCH CENTER/WASHINGTON, D.C.

GRC A-65 / P-364
February, 1980

The Glenmary Research Center was established in 1966 to help serve the research needs of the Catholic Church in rural America.

International Standard Book Number: 0-914422-10-3
Library of Congress Catalog Card Number: 79-55177

Published by the Glenmary Research Center, 4606 East-West Highway, Washington, D.C. 20014. $6.50

Contents

Tables

Maps

Preface

This book is the companion volume to our earlier *Atlas of Religious Change in America, 1952-1971* (Glenmary Research Center, 1978). It also represents the completion of more than four years of research collaboration. Our purpose here is to reach beyond a mere description of geographic patterns of denominational religion, to a social analysis of their causes and their consequences for changing patterns of religious regionalism, and cultural pluralism. We again thank both the National Science Foundation and the University of Connecticut Research Foundation for major funding over the past several years. The administrative talents of Florence Waxman, the typing skills of Barbara Brand, and the good humor of both have been of invaluable assistance. We are similarly grateful for the cartographic efforts of both Mark C. Nielson and Edesse Sloan, and the generous help of Chuck Monroe with numerous data processing tasks. Bernard Quinn, director of the Glenmary Center has been a loyal supporter of our work throughout. For both of us this project has meant the learning of a new field and the maturing of a friendship. Lastly, we again express our thanks to Fran and Judy. Obviously we alone are responsible for any errors or shortcomings herein.

William M. Newman
Peter L. Halvorson

1

The Social Analysis of American Religion

THE SCIENTIFIC STUDY OF RELIGION

In its best moments, science, like fiction, attempts to tell a story. This book provides a chapter in the story of American religion. As students of American religion are aware, the Constitutional separation of church and state prohibits government agencies from collecting information from citizens about their religion. Therefore, despite the very impressive growth of the social sciences since mid-century, and the accompanying proliferation of attitudinal and opinion surveys on religious ideas and practices, the absence of United States Census data has left a fundamental gap in our knowledge of American religious trends. It is true that in a brief period, between 1906 and 1936, the Census Bureau did undertake four special enumerations of church membership. However, the only instance in which the Bureau collected information about individual religious preferences was in 1957. A special population survey administered in that year gave rise to considerable controversy (Petersen 1962) that effectively closed the door to future such efforts. Ironically the 1957 current population survey of religion yielded relatively little detailed information of use to social scientists (United States Commerce Department 1958). By the time the passage of the 1967 Freedom of Information Act (Public Law 89-489) allowed private scholars access to the survey, much of the original data had already been discarded by the Bureau (Goldstein 1969; Mueller and Lane 1972). The net result is that, in the absence of comprehensive Census Bureau data for religious groups, the only information about religion published by government agencies consists of yearly, national level statistics for denominations taken from the National Council of Churches of Christ (NCCC) annual *Yearbook of Ameri-*

can and Canadian Churches.

The present study is occasioned by the existence of two privately conducted census-type studies of American religion. These two studies, which are described extensively in the next section of this chapter, are *Churches and Church Membership in the United States 1952*, sponsored by the NCCC, and a similar study for 1971 jointly sponsored by the Glenmary Research Center, NCCC, and the Lutheran Church, Missouri Synod (Whitman and Trimble 1954; Johnson, Picard and Quinn 1974). These two studies are unique in that they provide county (rather than merely national) level enumerations for a representative assortment of American religious denominations for both time periods. As such, they form an appropriate basis for a census-type examination of American religious trends over nearly a quarter of a century.

Our own collaborative work with these data has evolved in three stages, of which this book represents the final stage. As explained in detail elsewhere (Newman, Halvorson, and Brown 1977; Halvorson and Newman 1978a), it was first necessary to transform these two similar studies, and several related data sources, into a compatible time-series data archive. Begun in the summer of 1975, that task was eventually accomplished through the generous financial support of the National Science Foundation, the University of Connecticut Research Foundation, the Hartford Seminary Foundation and the United Church of Christ Board for Homeland Ministries. Once created, the data archive pointed in two directions. First, with the notable exception of geographer Wilbur Zelinsky's work (1961) with the 1952 data, nothing approaching a comprehensive denominational atlas had ever been attempted. More importantly, the absence of appropriate time-series data had forstalled the creation of an atlas of religious change patterns. Accordingly, our earlier book, *Atlas of Religious Change in America, 1952-1971* (1978b), marked the completion of the second phase of our work with these data. Its purpose was to depict relative patterns of geographic location and change for all available individual denominations. Additionally, the *Atlas* indicates places where changing distributions also mean changing denominational significance vis-a-vis other denominations. The *Atlas*, therefore, was intended to provide a definitive descriptive portrait of denominational religion in America from 1952 to 1971.

The present book is designed to be a companion volume which continues the scrutiny of these trends from precisely those points where the *Atlas* concludes. This is true in several senses. First, while the *Atlas* describes denominational patterns, little in the way of explanation or analysis is attempted. Thus a first concern of this book is to move beyond describing denominational trends to analyzing and explaining them. A second focus of this book is the aggregate religious trends for the 1952-1971 period. The final set of maps in the *Atlas* contains aggregate patterns for all denominations. This book expands and completes the analysis begun there. Here it is not denominational religion but the overarching issues of religious regionalism and pluralism that become the paramount concerns. Again, there have been few prior efforts of this type. Geographers, particularly Sopher (1967) and Shortridge (1976, 1977), have attempted relatively limited examinations of the aggregate 1952 and 1971 data separately. More recently, Carroll, Johnson, and Marty (1979) have offered some speculations about the 1950-1971 period, but have done so without the benefit of actual time-series change data. Obviously an analysis of general change patterns and their implications for the American religious landscape had to await the creation of a time-series data archive, which was the first phase of our work with these materials.

The remaining section of this chapter presents a detailed discussion of the creation of the data archive. Next, in a continuation of our descriptive portrait of denominational religion, Chapter 2 summarizes the broad trends emerging from the data. Chapter 3 marks the beginning of our analytical portrait. The idea of religious regionalism has long been a part of the attempt to understand composite patterns in American religion. Simply stated, most scholars assume that denominations are woven into distinctively regional patterns that reflect important differences in regional culture in the United States. The census-type data provide a rare opportunity to examine empirically the accuracy of these two assumptions. In Chapter 3, factor analytic techniques are used to detect statistical relationships among groups of denominations. The resulting typology reflects important historical, ethnic, and theological continuities in American religion. In Chapter 4, the regional components of that typology are examined. To a high degree American institutional religion exhibits clear regional patterns. However, these patterns differ from traditional views about America's cultural regions.

The subject of religious pluralism takes center stage in Chapter 5. Even with comprehensive denominational data and a viable regional typology based on them, changing patterns of pluralism remain a complex and elusive thing to measure. The several different approaches to this problem offered in this chapter underscore the limits of equating religious pluralism with cultural pluralism.

Chapter 6 addresses the social causes of the religious trends presented in the preceding chapters. Having provided a national portrait of religious change for the 1952-1971 period, the extent to which these patterns can be explained must be probed. Here we focus especially upon the role of broader social and economic variables, as provided by the United States Census data, in generating religious trends. The concluding chapter considers the implications of our findings for the conventional wisdom about religion in America. To what extent do these census-type data confirm or conflict with the images of American religion for this period previously constructed on the basis of survey-type studies?

THE ARCHIVE OF AMERICAN RELIGIOUS DENOMINATIONS

Empirical studies in the social sciences require a precise statement about the data and methodology. This study is no exception. Our goal is to provide a comprehensive picture of the sources and nature of the county level data upon which the book is based. Additionally, it is important at the outset to understand both the limitations of these data, and the ways in which we have modified the original materials to produce a reliable time-series data archive.

As stated earlier, during the early 1950s, the Bureau of Research and Survey of the NCCC took the unprecedented step of attempting to compile a county by county religious census of the United States. The resulting data cover 114 denominations, account for over 79 percent of the total national church membership reported in the 1952 NCCC *Yearbook*, and are essentially a county by county breakdown thereof. These statistics reflect information voluntarily provided by individual religious organizations. Like most first attempts, the data published in Lauris Whitman's and Glen Trimble's *Churches and Church Membership in the United States 1952* (1954) contain several important flaws.

The following are the major faults of the study, as already pinpointed in previous works (Newman, Halvorson, & Brown 1977, Halvorson & Newman 1978b). First, the data compiled include not simply statistics for the year 1952 but an assortment of figures for the years 1952 through 1954. Fortunately, the longer the time interval involved in time-series uses of these data, the less bothersome such "slippage" in the timeframe becomes. Second, Whitman and Trimble, relying entirely upon voluntary participation, where not able to impose membership criteria or enumeration methods upon individual denominations. It is widely recognized that different religious groups define membership differently. Whereas one denomination calls only adults members, another denomination's definition of "members" may include young children. Thus the membership figures for different groups are not necessarily comparable. Finally, many groups report both members and a larger category called "adherents." The latter typically includes individuals who participate infrequently but still are assumed to identify with the particular denomination or local congregation. For denominations reporting both counts the NCCC retained only the larger statistic. The 1952 study therefore contains a mixture of members statistics and adherents statistics, with no record made of which type was reported for each denomination.

Information so coarsely presented may raise questions about the value of such statistics. It must, however, be remembered that these county level figures were collected in exactly the same manner as the national level figures reported in the NCCC annual *Yearbook*. They are the same statistics routinely published on an annual basis by the United States Department of Commerce as authoritative in a myriad of government handbooks and reports. The only thing different about the 1952 study was that a unique effort was made to collect data at the more discrete county level, rather than simply the national level. Social scientists have cited these self-reported statistics almost as often as they have criticized them. After observing that "nothing is more elusive in church history than honest statistics," historian Franklin Littell turns to precisely these kinds of figures to build his case in *From State Church to Pluralism* (1962). These same NCCC *Yearbook* statistics also provide the point of departure for Herberg's classic *Protestant-Catholic-Jew* (1955). As already noted, the major scholarly use of the 1952 county level *Churches and Church Membership* study was by geographer Wilbur Zelinsky (1961). After comparing the 1952 study to the last United States Census Bureau enumeration of church membership done in 1936, Zelinsky concludes that the 1952 study is far closer to an accurate census than the earlier government study. The maps of major denominational families from the 1952 data produced by Zelinsky (1961) became standard reference documents for their field. Through Zelinsky's efforts and the subsequent use of these data by David Sopher in *Geography of Religions* (1967) and by Edwin Gaustad in his *Historical Atlas of Religion in America* (1962), the 1952 county level study, despite its shortcomings, became recognized as the most comprehensive census-type study of American religious membership ever undertaken.

Almost twenty years elapsed before anything like the 1952 study was again attempted. Perhaps the disenchantment of religious leaders with social science accounts for this lapse; there is little question that the two professions drew apart in the intervening years (Fukuyama 1963). In the late 1960s, the NCCC, the Lutheran Church—Missouri Synod, and the Glenmary Research Center (a Catholic agency) jointly sponsored a replication of the 1952 study. The result was the publication of *Churches and Church Membership in the United States 1971* (Johnson, Picard, and Quinn 1974).

The new study dovetails remarkably well with the earlier one. The 1971 study called upon church executives at regional, state, and county levels to double check the accuracy of their statistics before entering them into the data file. It is significant that the denominational statistics from both the 1952 and 1971 county level studies are quite consistent with aggregate NCCC *Yearbook* figures throughout the period. As will be seen, although the 1971 study contains only half as many denominations as the 1952 study, the participation of most major denominations in both time periods provides not only for compatibility between the data files, but also a high degree of representativeness in both studies.

As already noted, the 1952 study exhibited two major flaws: different criteria of membership were used by different denominations, and the statistics ultimately reported in the published study contained a mixture of member and adherent figures. The sponsors of the 1971 study were no more in a position than had been the NCCC earlier to dictate enumeration criteria to individual religious denominations. While one may question the comparability of statistics between denominations, it is probable that *within* any particular denomination between 1952 and 1971 the same methods of counting were used, and that denominational data are internally consistent. Additionally, the inconsistency of statistics between denominations is somewhat alleviated by the fact that part of the analysis in this book focuses not upon raw numbers for either 1952 or 1971, but upon change rates between the two time periods. This use of change rate data in effect creates a new internally consistent yardstick by which the performances of different denominations, employing different counting methods, may be accurately measured and compared.

However, the problem of members verses adherents remains. There is absolutely no way to avoid the fact that the 1952 denominational statistics are a mixture, and that we are unable to determine which groups reported which type of statistic. In the 1971 study, when denominations reported both members and adherents both figures are recorded. When groups reported only members, the adherents figures were estimated by procedures described in the study. Therefore, it must be decided whether to use 1971 members or adherents figures. We have opted for the adherents statistics for several reasons. First, Catholics account for over 40 percent of the respective data sets, and they report only the more inclusive adherents type of statistic. Given the numeric, cultural, and geographic significance of Catholicism, any analysis of American religious trends not including them would be woefully incomplete. This

TABLE 1

Denominations for Which 1952 and 1971 County Data Are Available

DENOMINATION	ADHERENTS 1952	ADHERENTS 1971	CHANGE IN ADHERENTS	PERCENT CHANGE
American Baptist U.S.A.	1 528 846	1 693 423	164 577	11
American Lutheran	1 744 142	2 490 537	746 395	43
Baptist General Conference	49 881	125 678	75 797	152
Brethren in Christ	6 046	11 458	5 412	90
Catholic	29 624 787	44 863 492	15 238 705	51
Christian Reformed	155 007	208 965	53 958	35
Church of the Brethren	189 277	220 813	31 536	17
Church of God (Anderson)	105 580	389 389	283 809	269
Church of God (Cleveland)	136 386	269 989	133 603	171
Church of the Nazarene	249 033	869 821	620 788	249
Cumberland Presbyterian	93 235	104 070	10 835	12
Episcopal	2 544 320	3 032 197	487 877	19
Evangelical Congregational	28 476	35 742	7 266	26
Evangelical Covenant	52 780	82 453	29 673	56
Free Methodist	49 052	63 540	14 488	30
Friends	95 499	131 771	36 272	38
International Foursquare Gospel	66 191	101 522	35 342	53
Jewish	5 112 024	6 113 520	1 001 496	20
Lutheran Church in America	2 481 927	3 010 150	528 223	21
Lutheran — Missouri Synod	1 856 633	2 772 996	916 363	49
Mennonite	66 900	108 108	41 208	62
Moravian — North and South	48 618	57 121	8 503	18
Mormons (West only)	822 700	2 016 590	1 193 890	145
N.A. Baptist General Conference	35 265	50 583	15 318	43
Pentecostal Holiness	41 555	89 140	47 585	115
Presbyterian U.S.	745 627	1 147 499	401 872	54
Reformed	194 157	370 509	176 352	91
Seventh-Day Adventist	252 554	536 082	283 528	112
Seventh-Day Baptist	6 435	6 178	-257	-4
Southern Baptist	8 121 069	14 488 635	6 367 566	78
Unitarian Universalist	159 904	194 733	34 829	22
UCC/Congregational	2 013 935	2 411 438	397 503	20
United Methodist/Evan. N.A.	9 512 669	11 523 749	2 011 080	21
United Presbyterian U.S.A.	2 670 167	3 546 941	876 774	33
Wisconsin Evan. Lutheran	316 642	381 920	65 278	21
Total	71 178 238	103 627 402		46

fact alone mandates using the more inclusive adherents figures. Second, the statistics for American Jews, derived in both time periods from the *American Jewish Yearbook* (American Jewish Committee), are also more compatible with adherent than with member statistics. Finally, our own personal preference was to risk overcounting some denominations rather than undercounting others. Consequently, the shortcomings of the 1971 data are offset by their comparability to the 1952 data, and by the unique opportunity that the two sets in conjunction provide for trend analyses.

Thus far we have described the circumstances under which the two census-type studies came into existence and some of the basic characteristics of the data contained in them. The task of creating a compatible time-series archive from those two studies and several supplemental data sources was a somewhat complex process. Table 1 presents the complete list of 35 denominations that comprise the 1952-1971 data archive to be used in this study. How did this particular listing of denominations come into being? How representative or inclusive a sampling of American religious groups is this listing? What are its omissions and limitations? Let us consider these questions in reverse order.

First, concerning possible omissions or limitations, virtually all the major Protestant groups, Catholics, and Jews are included in this archive. There are three major omissions. None of the primarily black denominations are represented in 1952 or 1971. Certain primarily white denominations, such as the Protestant Episcopal Church and the United Church of Christ, claim black adherence and there are, of course, substantial nonwhite members in the Catholic Church. Nevertheless, the portrait presented here is basically one of white religious groups in the United States. Additionally, two major branches of evangelical Protestantism are missing from the data, the Assemblies of God, and the Churches of Christ and Churches of God. These omissions probably result in an undercounting of religious affiliation in the South and Southwest, regions where these groups are known to be especially prevalent. Not only are all the remaining large Protestant groups included, but a remarkably diverse assortment of smaller denominations are also present. The number of specific religious denominations included here far exceeds that in any sample survey ever conducted in the United States.

Second, how representative or inclusive is this assort-

TABLE 2

Proportion of Total Church Membership and Total Population Represented in the Longitudinal Archive

	1952	1971	PERCENT CHANGE
Total Members	71 178 238	103 627 402	46
NCCC *Yearbook* Totals	87 027 507	124 829 551	43
Percent of Yearbook Totals	82	83	
Total U.S. White Population	134 874 138	178 197 190	32
Percent of U.S. White Population	53	58	
Total U.S. Population	150 697 361	203 212 877	35
Percent of U.S. Population	47	51	

NOTE: With the exception of the data taken from the NCCC *Yearbook*, all other data in this table are taken from the computer tape for the *Archive of American Religious Denominations 1952-1971*, compiled by William M. Newman and Peter L. Halvorson. The *Archive* tape is available from the Social Science Data Center of the University of Connecticut at Storrs.

ment of denominations? That question is most clearly answered in statistical terms. Table 2 shows the percent of NCCC *Yearbook* totals for 1952 and 1971 and of United States populations for 1950 and 1970 (the nearest census years) represented in the *Archive of American Religious Denominations*. In both 1952 and 1971 this *Archive* accounts for 82 percent or more of the total national religious adherence reported by the NCCC in its *Yearbook*. Such a proportion ensures that the religious data archive is sufficiently large and inclusive to be used for accurate trend analysis. This is further corroborated by the fact that in both 1952 and 1971 these data sets account for over half of the white population of the United States as reported in the 1950 and 1970 United States Census reports.

Finally, how was this particular assortment of denominations selected? A beginning was made by identifying those denominations that participated in both studies and that were not affected by either splits or mergers between 1952 and 1971. Next, adjustment was made for those denominations affected by splits and/or mergers. The easier cases simply required merging the 1952 county level statistics for those groups that actually merged with each other by 1971. As is shown in Table 3, the groups involved in this process were the American Lutheran Church (ALC), Lutheran Church in America (LCA), Missouri Lutherans, Mennonites, Unitarian Universalists, United Presbyterians, and Friends. This left two difficult cases to be resolved, involving both mergers and splits. The merger creating the United Church of Christ (UCC) resulted in a splinter group of Congregational Christian Churches. The only way to maintain compatibility between the 1952 and 1971 denominational figures in this case was to add the 1971 UCC and Congregational Christian data. The result approximated the 1952 merged data for the Evangelical and Reformed Church and the Congregational Christian Churches.

A more complex situation developed from the union of the United Methodist Church with the Evangelical United

Brethren. A group of Brethren churches objecting to that merger joined with the Holiness Methodist Church to create the Evangelical Church of North America. The best solution to this case was to create an artificial merger between the Brethren and the two Methodist bodies in 1952 and combine the United Methodists and Evangelical Church of North America in 1971. It will be seen that in both of the foregoing instances the option was for slight overcounting instead of creating artificial numerical and geographical shrinkage. While some records indicated that the 1952 study had at one time been entered onto IBM data cards, our search for them was fruitless. Therefore, we made the above described alterations in the 1952 data prior to the process of creating our own computer file of these statistics from the published reports.

TABLE 3

Denominations Requiring Aggregation and/or Addition because of Mergers and Schisms between 1952 and 1971

DENOMINATION	Adherents	
	1971	1952
American Lutheran	2 490 537	
American Lutheran		800 055
Evangelical Lutheran		895 138
United Evangelical Lutheran		48 952
Lutheran Church in America	3 010 150	
American Evangelical Lutheran		20 234
Augustana Evangelical Lutheran		433 106
Finnish Evangelical Lutheran		29 761
United Lutheran Church in America		1 998 826
Lutheran Church — Missouri Synod	2 772 996	
Lutheran Church — Missouri Synod		1 835 605
Slovak Evangelical Lutheran		21 028
Mennonite Church	108 108	
Mennonite Church		61 903
Conservative Mennonite Conference		4 997
Unitarian Universalist Association	197 733	
Unitarian Church		84 749
Universalist Church of America		75 155
United Church of Christ	2 305 229	
Congregational Christian Churches	106 209	
Congregational Christian Churches		1 263 472
Evangelical and Reformed		750 463
United Methodist	11 511 709	
Methodist		8 790 025
Evangelical United Brethren		722 966
Evangelical Church of N.A.	12 040	
Holiness Methodist		678
United Presbyterian U.S.A.	3 546 941	
Presbyterian U.S.A.		745 627
United Presbyterian of N.A.		221 918
Friends World Committee/America	131 771	
Rel. Soc. Friends, Conservative		1 993
Rel. Soc. Friends, Gen. Conference		16 650
Five Year Meeting of Friends		67 884
Rel. Soc. Friends, Philadelphia		3 748
Central Yearly Meeting of Friends		584
Oregon Yearly Meeting of Friends		4 680

NOTE: The Evangelical Church of North America was formed from a merger of the Holiness Methodist Church and members of the Evangelical United Brethren not participating in the EUB-Methodist Church merger. Since there is no way of counting the latter separately in the 1952 data set, we combined these denominations as United Methodist for both sets.

  Certain Congregationalists did not participate in the United Church of Christ merger. Thus, we added the 1971 Congregational Christian Churches with the United Church.

  The Moravian Church is disaggregated in the 1971 set into North and South groups. We combined the 1971 data into one denomination.

While statistics for American Jews were included in the 1952 study, they are absent from the 1971 research. Working from figures provided in the *American Jewish Year-book* (American Jewish Committee 1971) we created a county level data set for Jews. Since the figures in the 1952 study were taken from an earlier edition of that *Year-book*, the two data sets are entirely comparable. They differ somewhat from the other data used here because they are an estimation of Jewish population in communities containing 100 or more Jewish residents. However, these estimates are identical to those supplied to the NCCC *Yearbook* and are the only census-type statistics for American Jews.

A supplemental data set (Irvin 1976) compiled by the Southern Baptist Convention appeared to hold the promise of filling some gaps in the 1971 Study. However, as explained elsewhere (Halvorson and Newman 1978a), most of the data from that source proved to be unusable, although two small Protestant groups that participated in the 1952 study but not the 1971 study were derived from it. These are the International Church of the Foursquare Gospel and the Baptist General Conference. Finally, county level figures were available for Mormons in the 1952 study but not in 1971. Fortunately a privately collected 1971 data set for Mormons in the western states (Bennion 1976) became available. This has permitted inclusion of Mormons for that part of the nation where they are most numerous, but the incomplete nature of their data requires dropping them from certain types of analyses.

Three additional minor adjustments of the original data sources should be mentioned. First, based upon information supplied to us by the United Church of Christ, substantial corrections have been made in their statistics for some counties that were greatly underenumerated in the 1971 study. Second, we have combined the North and South reporting units of the Moravian church in 1971 to match the single reporting unit for 1952. Finally, while the 1952 study of the Jewish population provided individual statistics for the five counties (i.e. boroughs) of the New York metropolitan area, the 1971 study contained only a single combined figure. We have divided that latter statistic into five county level figures by estimating county level Jewish populations retroactively from a later data source (i.e. the 1976 edition of the *American Jewish Yearbook*). This then is how the final list of usable denominations was compiled for the trend analyses in this book.

Most of the work done by social scientists with quantitative data files involve sample surveys. Relatively few of us have the opportunity to do first-hand work with census or census-type data files. For its purposes the *Archive of American Religious Denominations* (see Halvorson and Newman 1978a), is a remarkably complete data source. Our own appreciation of the completeness of these religious data files stems in part from our concurrent work with the United States Census statistics that were also entered into the *Archive*. The United States Census Bureau does not, of course, claim to have counted every citizen. The Census is really an exceptionally accurate population estimate. Nevertheless, after a census study is completed, the Bureau spends a great deal of time and effort (essentially until the next Census is conducted) correcting errors in its study. Accordingly, instead of there being only one single authoritative United States Census report, the Bureau releases successive versions or revisions of each Census. Population counts may vary by the thousands for given counties from one version to the next. This process is not described in criticism of the United States Census Bureau, but rather to create an awareness of the limitations of any such study. All census-type enumerations are necessarily estimations. Against this background, the data for religious groups used here are uniquely accurate and complete, and surely provide a rare opportunity for the understanding of American religious trends.

2
A Closer Look at the 'Religious Revival'

THE MEANINGS OF NUMBERS

There appears to be general agreement among scholars that the late 1950s produced some form of religious revival in the United States. Of course, there has been substantial debate about the spiritual significance of America's "return to popular piety." Some writers warn that organizational growth should not be equated with a renewal of faith. Others maintain that the emergence of a rather bland "religion in general" or "civic religion" was responsible for the swelling of the membership rolls (Herberg, 1955; Hudson 1953; Marty 1958; Mead 1963). The aggregate statistics from the 1952-1971 data *Archive* at least confirm the fact that American mainstream denominational religion did experience an unprecedented spurt of growth. The 46 percent growth rate for religious groups between 1952 and 1971 compares impressively with the smaller 35 percent growth rate for the general population between 1950 and 1970 (see Tables 1 and 2).

Several features of the internal dynamics of these statistics warrant closer inspection. The overall rate of 46 percent masks a remarkably diverse assortment of change rates for the 35 individual denominations. These figures range from a low of -4 percent for the Seventh Day Baptists, to an impressive 269 percent growth rate for the Church of the Brethren. However, it must be remembered that absolute numbers and change rates, taken separately, can give very different pictures of the same events. Neither type of statistic can be meaningfully interpreted in the absence of the other. For example, the Church of the Brethren is a relatively small denomination. Its growth rate of 269 percent represents less than 250,000 new adherents. In contrast, the Episcopal Church reports one of the lowest growth rates of the dozen or so largest Protestant

denominations. Yet its 12 percent increase actually represents an influx of over 500,000 new adherents. Similarly, the modest growth figure of 21 percent for the United Methodist Church translates into over 2,000,000 new adherents.

In simple terms, the larger the denomination the more difficult for it to register an extremely high growth rate. Conversely, the smaller the denomination the greater the likelihood that small absolute gains will translate into impressive change rates. Thus when large groups, in these data, for example, both the Catholic Church and the Southern Baptist Convention, report relatively high change rates, such cases deserve careful attention. They tend to be the exception not the rule in these kinds of data.

Unfortunately the difference between absolute numbers and change rates are sometimes ignored in studies of religious trends. A case in point is Dean Kelley's widely read *Why Conservative Churches Are Growing* (1973). Kelley's theme is that the conservatism of a church's theology explains why it experienced high growth rates during these years. His argument is based upon an analysis of annual NCCC *Yearbook* statistics in percentage terms. Kelley is partly correct in that some of the success stories in American religion during this period are those of theologically conservative denominations. However, as will be seen later, our own county level data provide persuasive evidence for the view that social and historical variables, rather than conservative theology, explain these patterns. For the moment however, we wish merely to demonstrate that Kelley's focus upon percentages creates some very misleading images of the trends for the period.

For instance, Kelley shows (1973: 27) that between 1940 and 1969 the conservative branch of American Presbyterianism, the Presbyterian Church in the United States,

TABLE 4

County Statistics for All Denominations

DENOMINATION	1952	1971	PERCENT OF COUNTIES IN 1971 (N = 3073)	NET CHANGE	
				No.	Percent
American Baptist U.S.A.	1063	1058	34	−5	−0.5
American Lutheran	875	988	32	113	12.9
Baptist General Conference	170	277	9	107	62.9
Brethren in Christ	49	73	2	24	49.0
Catholic	2556	2817	92	261	10.2
Christian Reformed	122	181	6	59	48.4
Church of the Brethren	458	427	14	−31	−6.8
Church of God (Anderson)	988	993	32	5	0.5
Church of God (Cleveland)	1069	1482	48	413	38.6
Church of the Nazarene	1607	1733	56	126	7.8
Cumberland Presbyterian	303	288	9	−15	−5.0
Episcopal	1942	2033	66	91	4.7
Evangelical Congregational	31	30	1	−1	−3.2
Evangelical Covenant	246	262	9	16	6.5
Free Methodist	575	549	18	−26	−4.5
Friends	242	460	15	218	90.1
International Foursquare Gospel	288	350	11	62	21.5
Jewish	481	504	16	23	4.8
Lutheran Church in America	1039	1146	37	107	10.3
Lutheran — Missouri Synod	1421	1649	54	228	20.3
Mennonite	230	358	12	128	55.7
Moravian — North and South	50	53	2	3	6.0
N.A. Baptist General Conference	145	152	5	7	4.8
Pentecostal Holiness	368	489	16	121	32.9
Presbyterian U.S.	958	1035	34	77	8.0
Reformed	151	203	7	52	34.4
Southern Baptist	1784	2212	72	428	24.0
Seventh-Day Adventist	1462	1624	53	162	11.1
Seventh-Day Baptist	46	45	1	−1	−2.2
Unitarian Universalist	366	520	17	154	42.1
UCC/Congregational	1397	1296	42	−101	−7.2
United Methodist/Evan. N.A.	2881	2955	96	74	2.6
United Presbyterian U.S.A.	1831	1857	60	26	1.4
Wisconsin Evan. Lutheran	248	352	11	104	41.9

NOTE: Mormons are excluded due to lack of complete county level data.

reports an 80 percent increase, compared to only a 40 percent rate for the more liberal United Presbyterian Church in the USA. Similarly, our 1952-1971 data archive reports 54 and 33 percent change rates for these two groups respectively. Yet the United Presbyterian Church acquired just under 1,000,000 new adherents during this period, compared to less than 500,000 for the more conservative Presbyterian Church in the US. In other words, the more liberal (and numerically larger) denomination grew at almost half the rate of its conservative counterpart, but also acquired nearly twice the actual number of new adherents. Kelley's percentage graphs completely obscure the fact that the liberal denomination experienced far more actual numerical increase than did the conservative one.

A more dramatic illustration of the fallacy of measuring trends only in percentage terms is Kelley's comparison of the change rates for the United Methodist Church and a more conservative Methodist denomination, the Wesleyan Church. Kelley's graph for the 1940-1969 period shows the United Methodist Church growing at a 40 percent rate, compared to an impressive 90 percent for the Wesleyan Church. Interestingly, both denominations participated in mergers in 1968. In that year the total national adherence

of the merged Wesleyan Church was a mere 80,000. The merged United Methodist Church reported over 10,000,000 adherents. The Evangelical United Brethren (EUB) alone contributed over 750,000 adherents to that merger. Does it make much sense to compare the change rate of a denomination of over 10,000,000 adherents with that of another denomination numbering less than 100,000? While the time-series archive does not contain useable data for the Wesleyan Church, it seems clear that between 1952 and 1971 the United Methodists gained far more adherents than the total 1971 size of the smaller, more conservative denomination.

Most studies have shown that by the mid-1970s religious organizational growth trends were tapering into what would become a period of general decline rather than increase. In this context it becomes all the more dangerous to overstate the meanings of change rates without also considering the absolute numerical trends involved. We shall return to these issues, as well as the accuracy of the so-called "Kelley hypothesis," in later chapters. For the moment our purpose is to caution readers against overestimating the significance of the percentage figures in these or any other data. The absolute numerical significance of trends must not be overlooked.

TABLE 5

Index of Concentration for All Groups for the Continental United States 1952-1971

DENOMINATION	N = 3073 COUNTIES			N = COUNTIES WHERE PRESENT		
	1952	1971	Change	1952	1971	Change
American Baptist U.S.A.	.893	.882	−.009	.689	.657	−.032
American Lutheran	.898	.889	−.009	.640	.655	.015
Baptist General Conference	.977	.968	−.009	.582	.638	.056
Brethren in Christ	.995	.994	−.001	.694	.727	.033
Catholic	.890	.887	−.003	.868	.862	−.006
Christian Reformed	.990	.986	−.004	.752	.758	.006
Church of the Brethren	.952	.956	.004	.675	.685	.010
Church of God (Anderson)	.869	.873	.004	.593	.607	.014
Church of God (Cleveland)	.859	.831	−.028	.596	.634	.038
Church of the Nazarene	.804	.793	−.011	.624	.633	.009
Cumberland Presbyterian	.964	.963	−.001	.630	.607	−.023
Episcopal	.883	.862	−.021	.816	.791	−.025
Evangelical Congregational	.977	.997	−.020	.673	.666	−.007
Evangelical Covenant	.972	.967	−.005	.641	.607	−.034
Free Methodist	.972	.928	−.044	.559	.597	.038
Friends	.975	.952	−.023	.683	.676	−.007
International Foursquare Gospel	.978	.969	−.009	.762	.717	−.045
Jewish	.987	.985	.002	.918	.906	−.012
Lutheran Church in America	.915	.897	−.018	.748	.724	−.024
Lutheran—Missouri Synod	.880	.858	−.022	.740	.735	−.005
Mennonite	.981	.973	−.008	.744	.770	.026
Moravian—North and South	.995	.994	−.001	.674	.660	−.014
N. A. Baptist General Conference	.977	.977	.000	.518	.538	.020
Pentecostal Holiness	.985	.938	−.047	.564	.612	.048
Presbyterian U.S.	.907	.911	.004	.702	.735	.032
Reformed	.948	.981	.033	.699	.709	.010
Seventh-Day Adventist	.873	.865	−.008	.734	.745	.011
Seventh-Day Baptist	.994	.994	.000	.601	.567	−.034
Southern Baptist	.780	.772	−.008	.621	.682	.061
Unitarian Universalist	.890	.949	.059	.836	.700	−.136
UCC/Congregational	.882	.888	.006	.741	.734	−.007
United Methodist/Evan. N.A.	.638	.642	.006	.627	.627	.000
United Presbyterian U.S.A.	.854	.858	.004	.755	.765	.010
Wisconsin Evan. Lutheran	.976	.973	−.003	.706	.763	.057
Total U.S. Population	.684	.738	+.054			

NOTE: Mann-Whitney U-tests were performed in order to statistically compare the two sets of 1952 and 1971 Index of Concentration values. The values for U were 591 and 601 respectively. Those were converted to z scores of .159 and .282, neither of which approaches any conventional level of statistical significance. The F values resulting from the analyses of variance (.5252 and .0147 respectively) were not statistically significant at any accepted probability level.

Yet another complex aspect of these data is the relationship between growth in adherents and spatial change. As noted previously in the *Atlas*, when measured in terms of the number of county units occupied by a given denomination in the two time periods, spatial changes exhibit a smaller range of variability than do rates of change in adherents (as seen in Tables 3 and 4, from 90 percent to −7 percent, compared to a range of 269 percent to −4 percent). More importantly, it is difficult to claim that there is a correlation between these two kinds of change. Some 20 percent of the denominations grew in adherents while shrinking in geographic coverage. Again, disparities between absolute numbers and change rates are apparent, with the initial county coverage of a denomination in 1952 being of basic importance. Thus Roman Catholics acquire more "new" counties than any other denomination (261 counties). Yet because of their wide geographical distribution in 1952 they attain only a 10.2 percent spatial change rate.

Obviously, the more one compares simple tabular indices for the 35 denominations the more difficult it becomes to provide meaningful statements about general trends. In this sense much of this book describes a search for summary type statistics and higher levels of aggregation of these denominational data, both of which provide clarification of distinct trends. However, there are at least a few basic patterns that emerge from these data regardless of whether one examines denominational or aggregate statistics, and regardless of whether information is depicted cartographically or statistically. A brief examination of these trends sets the stage for the analyses offered in later chapters.

SUMMARIZING BASIC TRENDS

For the 1952-1971 period, American religious patterns exhibit remarkable stability. While surely the religious revival produced impressive changes in the magnitudes of both denominational and total religious adherence statistics, the general shape of America's religious landscape did not change much. Moreover, the rigidity of patterns of religion in an age of immense general population movement represents something of a counter-trend. If nothing else, the failure of religious groups to precisely mirror population shifts suggests that something more than demographic shift is involved in the numerical behavior of a religious denomination. In an age of sociological reductionism, that fact should provide some comfort to church leaders and theologians. The 1952 and 1971 denominational distribution maps in the *Atlas* repeatedly illustrate these basic facts. Few denominations exhibit major geographic shifts.

For the present analysis we have calculated a summary statistic called an index of concentration. The index may be thought of as a statistical summary of the cartographic patterns provided in the *Atlas*, and allows inspection of several related basic trends in the data. The index is based on a Lorenz curve. Essentially it measures the extent to which a denomination's geographic distribution of adherents departs from a hypothetically even distribution showing equal representation in all counties. The index ranges from a value of 1 to 0, with values close to 1 indicating maximum levels of concentration, i.e. most of a denomination's adherents in a relatively small number of counties. Conversely, numbers close to 0 indicate a very even distribution of a denomination's adherents across the available county units. The index thus calculated, for both the religious denominations and for the general United States population, as well as changes in the statistics between 1952 and 1971, allow the simultaneous inspection of several related basic trends in the data (see Table 5). In the present case the index has been calculated in two different ways. First, the index was calculated for each denomination for each time period on the basis of all 3073 available counties in the United States. Like the maps in the *Atlas*, these index numbers (the three lefthand columns in Table 5) emphasize the fact that most denominations occupy relatively limited geographical turf in strength. From the national perspective most denominations are highly concentrated, as is indicated by very high index numbers. However, in order to provide a more accurate picture of the internal characteristics of denominational patterns, the index has also been calculated for each denomination using only those counties within which it is located in the two time periods. This set of index numbers (the three righthand columns in Table 5) depicts not the national situation of a denomination, but its performance vis-a-vis its own geographic distribution.

We turn now to a more complete examination of the national statistics for the index of concentration, i.e. those based upon all 3073 counties. As already noted, since most denominations are relatively small, and located in relatively few counties, the first set of statistics in Table 5 are uniformly high. Significantly, only one denomination, the United Methodist Church, has an index number below .77. It is also the only denomination showing less spatial concentration than the general United States population (.638 as compared to .684). This finding is consistent with

Zelinsky's claim (1961), based on the 1952 data, that Methodism is unique in the national character of its distribution. Of course, it is hardly surprising that most denominations have higher degrees of concentration than the United States population. However, there are a dozen or so groups for which one might have predicted the reverse. Groups reporting memberships in the millions—Catholics, Jews, Episcopalians, United Presbyterians, the United Church of Christ, and the three major Lutheran bodies— are also significantly more concentrated than the United States population. The statistics for these groups clearly indicate that American denominational religion is characterized by geographic liminality. Stated differently, even when large numbers of adherents and counties are involved, truly significant concentrations of any single denomination exist only in limited numbers of counties. Apparently the only exception to that general rule is Methodism.

More importantly, a comparison of these national level indices for 1952 and 1971 indicates overwhelming stability. Only 11 of the 35 religious groups register as much as .010 change in either direction on the index. In other words, the largest shifts in the index are only one percent of the measurement scale of the index. This pattern of stability in the geographic distributions of religious groups occurs in the face of a continuing trend toward increasing levels of geographic concentration of the general United States population. Isard (1960: 263) has demonstrated this general trend for the 1910-1950 period. Table 5 contains a calculation of this index for population for the 1952-1971 period. Obviously most denominations simply do not register changes approaching the magnitude of that for the general population. Moreover, religious groups do not uniformly follow population trends in terms of the directionality of change in this index. While a visual inspection of these statistics suggests that the 1952 and 1971 figures are not very different, it is also possible to test that impression statistically. A Mann-Whitney U-test and an analysis of variance, both of which essentially test for the statistical significance of differences in the two sets of index numbers, were performed. As anticipated, the result indicated no significant differences between the 1952 and 1971 index numbers for religious groups, and in this case no statistical difference indicates the essential sameness of the two data sets.

The second set of indices were calculated not on the basis of all counties, but only those counties within which each denomination was actually present. These numbers indicate the degree to which the denominations are "internally" concentrated within their own regions, and the degree to which regional "core areas" may be changing. These statistics for both dates are consistently of a lower order of magnitude than those calculated at the national level for all 3073 counties. As all values are above .500, there is still a clear tendency toward high levels of concentration for all the groups. It is particularly significant that the two groups

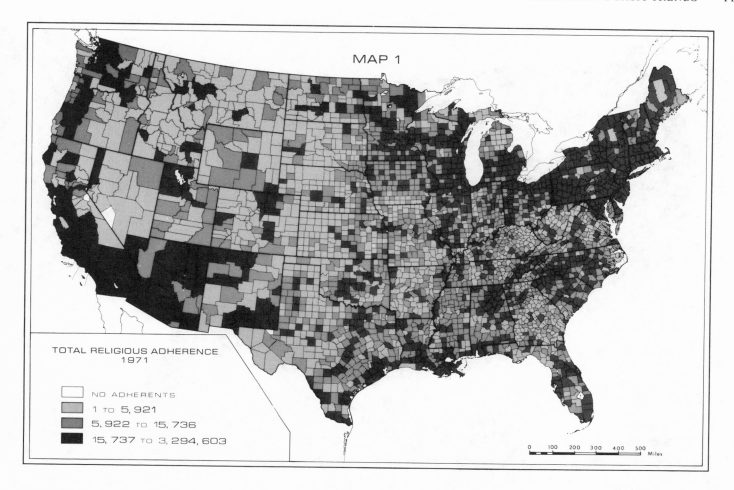

MAP 1

TOTAL RELIGIOUS ADHERENCE
1971

NO ADHERENTS
1 TO 5,921
5,922 TO 15,736
15,737 TO 3,294,603

0 100 200 300 400 500
Miles

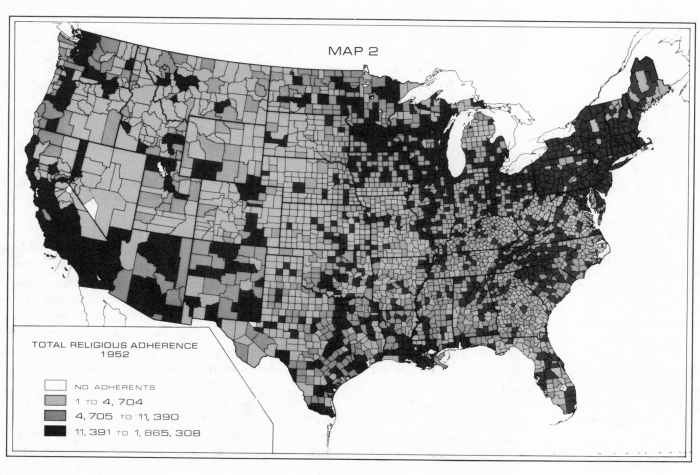

MAP 2

TOTAL RELIGIOUS ADHERENCE
1952

NO ADHERENTS
1 TO 4,704
4,705 TO 11,390
11,391 TO 1,865,308

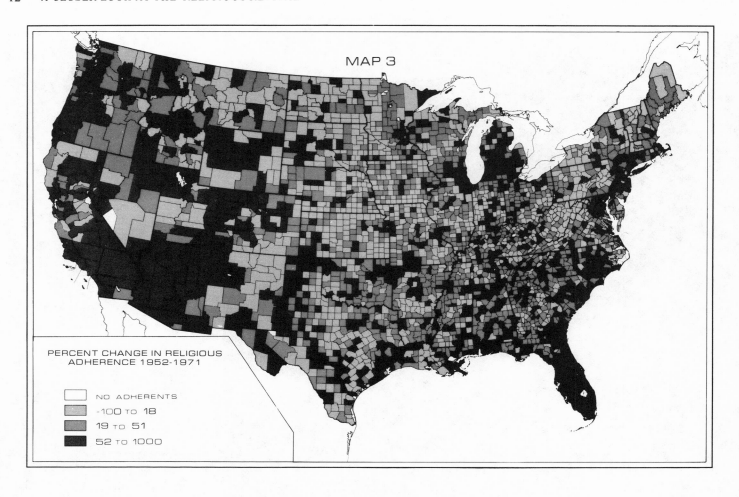

MAP 3

PERCENT CHANGE IN RELIGIOUS
ADHERENCE 1952-1971

- NO ADHERENTS
- -100 TO 18
- 19 TO 51
- 52 TO 1000

with the highest levels of concentration are Catholics and Jews. The fact that two such large and distinctive groups remain so internally concentrated may well account for, or be accounted for by, dominant social attitudes with regard to those groups. A detailed analysis of the data for American Jews is provided elsewhere (Newman and Halvorson 1979). Conversely, among the groups that are least concentrated none are very large, with only the two Churches of God having as many as 100,000 adherents. Thus, when viewed in terms of their internal distribution, while a wider range of variation is apparent, all groups exhibit relatively high degrees of concentration.

The pattern of change from 1952 to 1971 is a bit less clear when viewed from this internal perspective. There is more variability in the two indices. Four denominations have shifted by as much as .050 while eight experienced changes of less than .010. Among the strong shifts, the Southern Baptists are the most notable because, despite strong numerical growth and spatial expansion, they were more concentrated in 1971 than in 1952. But again, the dominant pattern is one of only minor change. Significance testing again indicated that the scores from 1952 to 1971 were not statistically different (see Table 5).

As noted at the outset, the statistics for the index of concentration for the 35 denominations presented in Table 5 reinforce the visual impressions one gets from inspecting the 1952 and 1971 maps for these groups presented in the

Atlas. These statistics, however, have the advantage of yielding rather precise numerical measurement and allow for testing some of the basic impressions gleaned from the denominational maps in the *Atlas.* Having established the overriding stability of the relative distribution of denominations between 1952 and 1971, it next seems appropriate to again provide a visual depiction of the combined effect of these denominational trends. In this regard at least, denominational and aggregate religious trends differ little from each other.

A cursory inspection of Maps 1, 2 and 3 leaves little question that the overall patterns of American religion closely follow the more general patterns of population. Map 1 portrays the aggregate pattern of total adherents in 1971 and clearly is best understood as a surrogate of the basic population distribution of the country. The map depicts total adherents in a trichotomy of categories, each containing the same number of counties. It should be noted that a few counties contain no population and are left blank. Thus, for ease of interpretation the map shows upper, middle and lower thirds, although the range within the categories is quite variable, with the upper category being particularly broad.

The upper third category is clearly concentrated in the northeastern quadrant of the country with secondary clusters in such areas as the Piedmont of the Southeast, Florida and the Gulf Coast, the Southwest (Arizona and

California), and the northwestern cluster in Washington and Oregon. Conversely, the lower third representing counties with less than about 6000 adherents is concentrated in the interior, particularly in the Great Plains and Mountain States of the western half of the country. Minor secondary pockets are found in the Central Appalachians, Central Georgia, and the Ozarks. These configurations of both strength and weakness in the pattern of religious adherents are entirely consistent with general population patterns for the country as revealed by the 1970 census.

The total adherents map for 1952 displays a pattern almost identical to that described for 1971. Although the category limits have shifted upward markedly from 1952 to 1971, one must inspect the maps very carefully to identify differences in the two distributions. Within the highest category, a small number of downward shifts appear to have occurred from 1952 to 1971 in the Northeast, while some upward shifts can be seen in the South and West. However, the general distribution of this category is very consistent on the two maps. The lower third category is found primarily in the western half of the country with the stated few small pockets in the eastern portion of the country. Thus, the overall impression is one of great consistency and, therefore, of great relative geographic stability despite the overall increases in the number of adherents.

Similarly, Map 3 depicting percent change in total adherents appears to correlate strongly with general patterns of population change. The highest category of change has a lower limit of 52 percent, indicating that one-third of the counties experienced significant growth in religious adherents during the period. Many of the counties in this category are located in the "Sun Belt" where high religious growth rates coincide with dynamic economic growth and substantial in-migration. Typical areas are the Gulf Coast and Florida, urban counties in the Piedmont, Tennessee and Texas, population centers in Colorado and Arizona, and West Coast communities. In the North and East such counties are less common and are mostly associated with urban clusters of major proportions, such as the corridors from New York to Washington, D.C. and around the southern Great Lakes. The lowest category here could include religious growth rates up to 18 percent, about half that of the national population growth rate. However, it is important to recall that large numbers of counties, particularly in more rural agricultural areas, actually declined in population during this period. It is not surprising then that this category appears frequently in such areas as the Great Plains, the upper Great Lakes region, Appalachia and the rural Southeast. This category is also common in much of upstate New York, New England, and in the Mountain States, where population levels have been relatively stable. In sum, the pattern of change in total religious adherence is different from the pattern of absolute incidence in 1971 and also highly consistent with patterns of general population change in the country for the period from 1950 to 1970.

In summary, two themes have been developed in this chapter. First, some of the basic trends emerging from the 1952-1971 *Archive of American Religious Denominations* have been depicted both statistically and cartographically. While absolute numerical increases indicate that there was a revival of joining among mainstream denominations, that revival did not greatly change the relative distributions of most individual denominations or the aggregate religious patterns. Thus several measures and depictions of these data exhibit stability far more than change. Additionally, it has been shown that the aggregate religious pattern in the United States for the 1952-1971 period strongly resembles that of the general population.

The second major theme of the chapter has been the limits of analyses at the denominational level. With some 35 individual denominations represented in two time periods, and an assortment of types of absolute numerical and change rate statistics, one's ability to speak in clear, general trend-like terms is circumscribed. For instance, absolute growth figures and change rates sometimes give completely different, even conflicting, impressions of what happened. Spatial change rates and numerical change rates do not cohere into a clear pattern for the 35 denominations. Some form of typology is required. Such a typology should combine individual denominational data into collective patterns more amenable to general trend analysis. These concerns are the focus of Chapters 3 and 4. However, before turning to that analysis, one additional implication of the data presented in this chapter warrants discussion.

It has been shown that American denominations experienced unprecedented growth rates during the period of the so-called religious revival. With these rates falling precipitously by the mid-1970s, church executives and other religious leaders began to express concern about the hows and whys of church growth and decline. The widespread discussion of Kelley's work (1972) was but one manifestation of this concern. The data for the 1952-1971 period examined in this chapter contain an important lesson about institutional growth. Although it is clear that religious change rates and population change rates appear highly correlated, the question of where religious institutions experienced the strongest absolute growth is not answered by change rate information. As was noted above, absolute numbers and change rate statistics can give completely different impressions of the same events. This is true in part because slight absolute increases create large percentage changes where the original absolute numbers are small. Both the index of concentration (Table 5) and the 1952 and 1971 base maps address this issue. Obviously American religion in the aggregate (compare the maps), as well as most denominations (read the index of concentration), acquired the most new adherents by 1971 in precisely those places that had the most adherents in 1952. Religious organizations grew most impressively where they were already strong. All of the various indices of geographic stability for the 1952-1971 period lead to this conclusion. Thus while patterns of geographic change, such as those presented in our earlier *Atlas*, are inherently interesting, for most denominations these patterns have rather slight absolute numerical consequences.

3

The Web of Denominationalism

IN SEARCH OF A TYPOLOGY

As has been seen in the preceding chapter, denominational statistics often appear to be a myriad of discrete and even conflicting indices. Beyond a few very basic trends it becomes increasingly difficult to offer meaningful generalizations based upon figures for the 35 individual denominations. The obvious solution to this problem is to select some form of typology or classification system by which denominations may be placed in meaningful groupings. Such a typology would hopefully bring together denominations having similar geographic distributions and change characteristics, thus clarifying general level patterns and trends for the 1952-1971 period. Is such a typology readily available?

Classification is a basic step in all science, and the disciplines of geography and sociology offer several different kinds of typologies of religious groups. For instance, much sociological literature focuses upon the distinction between church and sect. The church type of religious organization is depicted as large in size, providing substantial reinforcement for the surrounding societal values, and enjoys the position of *the* established religion. Conversely, the sect is understood to be generally smaller, offering strong opposition to the prevailing cultural norms, and consequently is seen as a marginal or deviant religious organization. As numerous authors have observed (Swatos 1976), most American religious bodies fall precisely in the middle between these two polar types of religious organization. As scholars from H. Richard Niebuhr (1929) to Franklin Littell (1962) have shown, American religious pluralism together with the official separation of church and state has lead to the spawning of *denominations*, which are neither church nor sect. American society boasts a diverse

spectrum of widely-subscribed denominations and our purpose here is to detect patterns in that denominationalism. Clearly such distinctions as church and sect, while useful in other contexts, will not be especially helpful here.

Much of the survey research conducted on American religion has relied upon a typology first introduced by sociologists Glock and Stark (1965). This typology appears in a variety of specific forms but generally divides denominations into broad liberal-moderate-conservative social and religious categories. Episcopalians, Congregationalists (now UCC), Unitarians, and Jews are usually defined as liberals. The moderates include the United Methodists, most Presbyterians, the ALC and LCA Lutheran bodies, and Catholics. Lastly, the conservatives include the Missouri Synod Lutherans, the Southern Baptists, and many of the evangelical Protestant bodies. Some alternate versions of the typology include both Fundamentalist and Sectarian categories.

Many studies demonstrate correlations between these religious groupings and people's attitudes on social and political issues. Views on social welfare policies, political party preference, and racial and ethnic attitudes are but a few of the categories studied in relation to these religious groupings. Unfortunately there is little precedent for using this typology in the study of geographical patterns of American religion. A few sociological studies (Knoke 1974; Grupp and Newman 1973) indicate some geographic orientation to this typology. However, the geographic categories used by these researchers are far less specific or exact than those commonly used by social geographers. Also, one of the few attempts to use a version of the Glock-Stark typology by a social geographer raises a number of bothersome methodological issues. We shall look closely at that study shortly. For the moment, it seems premature to adopt that typology for our present purposes.

Of course, it is impossible to think of typologies in geographical terms without introducing the notion of *regionalism*. The idea that there are significant regional differences on America's religious landscape, and that these differences articulate with cultural features of regions, seems to be a basic assumption of many social scientists. Understandably, given the absence of United States Census data on American religion, there have been few empirical studies of religious regionalism by social geographers. There are but three previous such studies. Zelinsky (1961) has undertaken an extensive exploration of the regional characteristics of the original data file for the 1952 NCCC study. Sopher (1967) provides a somewhat different depiction of these same data. Finally, Shortridge (1977) has undertaken a limited examination of the regional characteristics of the original 1971 church membership data. After examination, we decided not to adopt any of these three typologies, but a careful consideration of them does lead us to an innovative solution to the question of typology. As is often the case in science, the apparent errors of previous researchers are of inestimable value in providing a breakthrough. In this case, our critique of the efforts of both Zelinsky and Shortridge provide the solution to a dual problem, since obviously the issue of regionalism and the search for a typology are one and the same problem. If the memberships of denominations exhibit statistical associations, those patterns provide an appropriate typology by which trends may be illustrated. Let us then take a closer look at the regional hypothesis.

The assertion that American religion is highly regionalized rests on two different claims, both of which may be tested empirically with the kinds of data provided by the 1952 and 1971 church membership studies. The first testable hypothesis involved in the idea of regionalism is that groups of denominations exhibit geographic distributions in which there are strong statistical correlations among their memberships. For example, Southern Baptists and United Methodists have their strongest concentrations of adherents in the same places (i.e. the same counties). The second hypothesis is that these groups of statistically associated denominations occupy distinct geographic turfs or regions. This means, to stay with our example, that the geographic area in which Southern Baptists and United Methodists have their strongest combined adherence figures is not also occupied by any other set of denominations, and that this area may easily be identified as a cultural region, in this case the South. Unfortunately, previous researchers have failed actually to test the first of these hypotheses. Rather, some major assumptions have been made about the ways in which denominations are related. From such assumptions much of their works have become a self-fulfilling prophecy, in which those wanting to see religious-cultural regions have indeed seen them. In this chapter, the first of these two hypotheses will be tested, and a new typology of religious groups will be presented.

Subsequently, in the following chapter the geographic or regional component will be explored.

The analysis of the several previous regional typologies sets the stage for the new typology presented in this chapter. As is shown in Table 6, Zelinsky has proposed a typology of seven major religious regions and five subregions. As he explains it, the subregions appear as pockets within the regions, but differ from the regional patterns in terms of the major religious groups occupying that turf. In assessing Zelinsky's efforts, it is perhaps important to recall that his statistical and cartographic manipulation of this extremely large data file was accomplished manually, not by automated computer techniques. Since the late 1960s,

TABLE 6

**Religious Regions of the United States
as Proposed by Zelinsky**

REGION/SUBREGION	DENOMINATIONAL COMPOSITION
New England	Major: Catholic, Congregational (UCC), Unitarian, Episcopal Minor: Jewish, Baptist
Mid-Atlantic	Major: Methodist, Catholic, Presbyterian, Baptist, Disciples of Christ, Episcopal Minor: Germanic sub-region in Pennsylvania, Maryland, Virginia and West Virginia
Upper Midwest	Major: Lutheran, Catholic, Congregational, Unitarian Minor: Methodist, Episcopal, Presbyterian, and smaller nativist and Germanic bodies.
Southern	Major: Baptist, Methodist, Presbyterian, Episcopal Minor: Native American Churches including Disciples of Christ, Church of the Nazarene and Church of God Subregions: German and Spanish Catholics in Texas; French Catholics in Louisiana and Florida Subregion: Carolina Piedmont, composed of Presbyterian, Congregational and Friends
Mormon Region (West Central)	Major: Mormon Minor: Catholic, Jewish, various Protestant groups
Spanish Catholic (Southwest)	Major: Catholic Minor: Baptist, Methodist, various British and native Protestant groups.
Western	Highly mixed; strong area for Adventists, some areas of Catholic strength; much like both upper Midwest and New England

NOTE: This compilation and summary of Zelinsky's typology is taken from Zelinsky 1961: 163-164; 1973: 94-100.

computers have greatly expanded the techniques available for such analyses. How did he arrive at this regional typology? His seven major regions correspond precisely to the standard regions that social geographers have used in studying a wide variety of cultural and physical geographic characteristics. Unfortunately, no one (Zelinsky included) has demonstrated that clear statistical associations among denominations exist, and in turn fit these traditional culture regions. In Zelinsky's own words, "Most of the seven major regions and five subregions...can be justified neither by rigorous statistical logic nor by any obvious manifestations in the works or non-religious ways of men, but only by a certain loose areal association among certain groupings of church members, i.e. some moderate degree of homogeneity apparent to the map analyst" (1961:163).

As the footnote to Zelinsky's statement explains, relative ranks or densities of denominations were visually examined vis-a-vis assumed culture regions. It is hardly surprising then that the regional patterns of religion depicted cartographically by Zelinsky, and by Sopher as well, conform to prevailing popular images of regional culture in the United States. The typology of culture regions was the guiding pattern by which denominational families (Zelinsky) or individual denominations (Sopher) were assigned "moderate" association. There was no logical statistical testing of the associations of denominations or families of denominations with each other on any basis.

Scrutiny of the denominational make-up of Zelinsky's regions reveals yet another feature of his typology. The denominational groupings assigned to these culture regions overlap with one another repeatedly. Again, in Zelinsky's own words, "There is a great deal of heterogeneity within the postulated religious regions in terms of the lesser details of the areal patterns of individual denominational groups" (1961:165). In simple terms, Zelinsky is saying, for example, that Lutherans are clearly the dominant force in the upper Midwest, but beyond that, the upper Midwest contains an assortment of denominations similar to several other so-called regions.

By now it should be clear why we have chosen not to adopt Zelinsky's typology. First, he never tested the idea that there are statistical correlations between the geographic locations of memberships of denominations. He only undertook a rough bird's-eye view of these possible relationships. Second, he adopted an established typology of culture regions without in any way testing the empirical relationships of religious groups to that typology. Lastly, the religious compositions of some of the resulting regions overlap with one another in many ways. For our present purposes Zelinsky's work is of value because his assumptions all point to issues that ought to be empirically tested. Said differently, he has raised all of the key questions one ought to ask in order to arrive at an empirically generated typology of religious-geographic groups. However, he has not provided statistically precise, empirically validated answers to those questions.

There is little need to review in detail the work of David Sopher with these same data. Sopher (1967) has adopted the general cast of Zelinsky's work, but has attempted to identify more clearly the particular pockets of strength of individual denominations within that broad regional schema. His work adds little beyond this in terms of either methods or findings. His map of the data provides an interesting contrast to Zelinsky in one major respect. Zelinsky combined denominations into families, for instance,

treating all Lutherans as a category. Sopher retains individual denominations as units of analysis.

In contrast to the efforts of Zelinsky and Sopher, a very different methodological approach called cluster analysis is used by Shortridge. Working with the original data file from the 1971 church membership study, Shortridge arrives at what he calls a "new regionalization" of American denominations. Yet, as Shortridge himself observes, there is "remarkable similarity" between his five regions and

TABLE 7

Religious Regions of the United States as Proposed by Shortridge

RELIGIOUS COMPOSITION	PRIMARY LOCATION
1. Transitional	Scattered widely, but with some concentration in the upland South
2. Intense Conservative Protestant	Southeastern states (Baptists), Utah and adjacent states (Mormons), and northern Plains states
3. Diverse Liberal Protestant	Midwest and West Coast
4. Catholic	Northeast, upper Midwest, and metropolitan areas
5. Super Catholic	French Louisiana, Spanish Southwest (Texas, New Mexico, and Arizona)

NOTE: This summary of Shortridge's typology is taken from Shortridge (1977: 149-150).

those previously proposed by Zelinsky. Shortridge's regional typology appears in Table 7, and a visual inspection of it does confirm his claim that it is quite similar to that of Zelinsky. At the outset, it seems remarkable that, through rather complex computer techniques, he arrives at a typology for the 1971 data so similar to that created by Zelinsky through mere visual inspection of the earlier 1952 data. Indeed, much science is based upon replication and these two studies seem to establish verification for each other through such replication. On the other hand, one must not be mystified by modern computer techniques. Their prime advantage is that they allow high-speed computations in complex data management situations. But computer techniques are no better than the categories of analysis programmed into them. As will next be demonstrated, the particular approach to the cluster analysis technique used by Shortridge is little more than an automated version of the same untested assumptions employed by Zelinsky, which explains why the two studies produce such similar results.

The computer technique called cluster analysis is designed to simultaneously examine a large number of variables and to sort them into groups according to the strength of the relationships between those variables. In the present case, religious denominations are the variables involved, and the strengths of their memberships across the 3073 county units are the relationships that the computer is asked to examine and sort. In other words, ostensibly the cluster analysis is a very appropriate technique for testing the hypotheses that such statistical associations between denominations exist, and that they fall into a limited number of regional groupings. However, there are several problematic aspects of Shortridge's use of the cluster analysis technique.

Shortridge has not allowed individual denominations to serve as the variables to be examined by the cluster analysis technique. He has not empirically tested for statistical patterns among the geographical distributions of the 53 denominations contained in the original 1971 study. Rather he has programmed the computer to redefine the 53 denominations according to four criteria. Let us look at how he has converted the 53 denominational variables into four categories of religious variables.

First, he treats Catholic adherence not as one of 53 potentially associated denominational variables, but as one of four major criteria for defining the religious identities of counties. By treating Catholic adherence as a different class of variable than adherence in the remaining 52 Protestant groups, he has predetermined the existence of distinct Catholic regions. Since nearly 50 percent of all adherents in the 1971 data file are Catholics, it is not surprising that Shortridge's two regions, "Catholic" and "Super Catholic," correspond to the regions of Catholic density visually identified by Zelinsky and Sopher. That "finding" was created the moment that Catholic adherence became one of the four interpretive criteria provided for the cluster analysis.

Having separated Catholics from Protestants, Shortridge next provides three criteria by which the Protestant denominations will be associated. First, he distinguishes liberals from conservatives. There are two flaws in doing so. His distinction ignores a widely recognized range of more complex theological differences between denominations, liturgical vs. non-liturgical, liberal vs. neo-orthodox vs. conservative, and so on. More importantly, his distinction between liberal and conservative could perhaps better be labeled evangelical and non-evangelical, since membership in either the National Council of Churches or the National Association of Evangelicals is the actual measure employed (Shortridge 1976). The effect is to define as one grouping the 19th century extensions of Methodism and Baptism, plus arbitrarily, the various Lutheran immigrant groups. The operational result of the liberal-conservative distinction simply confirms the historic culture regions that evolved from the *original* settlement of these groups. In other words, it is not surprising that Shortridge "discovers" that religious groups fit culture regions that are so similar to those postulated by Zelinsky. His liberal-conservative criteria for identifying denominations is but a surrogate measure of these assumed historic culture regions.

This framework not only contradicts some important theological differences between groups, but entirely ignores various social criteria that have been identified as strong causal elements in patterns of religious adherence (Niebuhr 1929, Greeley 1972). The third criterion, religious intensity, is based upon Stark and Glock's typology, in this case a later version of it from the book *American Piety* (1968). In our view, this is little more than an alternative measure of the degree of evangelicalism, or what most researchers call "doctrinal orthodoxy." Its function here is to reinforce the liberal-conservative dichotomy used by Shortridge. Though different in name, these two sets of criteria reshape the denominational data in the same directions. The fourth criterion employed is the numerical dominance or denominational mix (Shortridge says "degree of pluralism") at the county level. It is our contention that the last of these four criteria is the one that should prevail and be empirically tested.

In summary, while Shortridge is to be credited for using the 1971 data to examine patterns of religious regionalism, his error lies in relying upon four powerful assumptions about the significance or meanings of denominational memberships, rather than examining and testing the statistical associations among them. An alternative way of conceptualizing the problem is to suggest that Shortridge has not really used religious denominations as variables having face validity. In their place he has introduced extraneous criteria with which denominational patterns may be redefined. He has not mapped the geographic patterns of statistically associated religious denominations. Instead he has mapped county units that exhibit four dichotomous religious variables alleged to be represented by denominational entities.

One last aspect of Shortridge's cluster analysis technique should be noted. The technique requires researchers to specify the number of groupings into which the variables will be sorted. That prejudgment about how many religious regions will ultimately be depicted seems to be but one additional device for pushing the data in the direction of the expected result.

Thus far in this chapter, certain diverse and complex methodological issues have been treated. Before proceeding, it seems of value to clarify once again the key issues that should guide any attempt to test the idea that denominations exhibit distinct patterns of relationship on some sort of geographic basis. First, no assumption should be made about how denominations are related. Instead, appropriate data-processing techniques should be used to see if meaningful statistical associations exist between denominations. The idea that these relationships are geographically regional can be examined once it is known whether or not the data sort into some form of typology. In fact, there is a data processing technique similar to that used by Shortridge that will allow these hypotheses to be tested.

AN EMERGING PATTERN

If one assumes that geographic patterns of denominational adherence may be granted face validity as measures of religion, then one may also test for the existence of statistically significant associations among such measures. As King and Hunt (1967, 1972) have demonstrated for attitudinal and reported behavioral measures of religiosity, factor analysis techniques are ideally suited for such tests. Factor analysis techniques are very similar in nature to the cluster analysis techniques used by Shortridge. Both procedures enable the computer to identify multiple statistical relationships between variables, and place those variables in groupings (alternately called cluster groupings and factor groupings) exhibiting the strongest statistical relationships. Both techniques allow researchers to examine complex statistical relations that would require inordinate time and effort to study by simple visual methods.

The logic for using factor analysis techniques with these data is as follows. Suppose one wants to know if those counties in which denomination A has its larger numbers of adherents are the same counties in which denomination B has its membership strengths. A simple correlational statistic (such as Pearson's r) answers that question. Of course, the situation confronting us here is much more complex because there are 35 denominations, not just two of them. Factor analysis techniques allow measurement of the multiple statistical correlations among the 35 denominations throughout the 3073 counties in the nation. Denominations whose patterns of geographical distribution are most similar to each other are placed in sets called factor groupings. A statistic called a factor loading is a summary measure of the strength of the correlation of any one denomination with all other denominations in its factor grouping. In this way the factor analysis technique tests the hypothesis that such relationships exist among these religious groups. Stated differently, we are testing the idea that certain underlying elements (or factors) tie together religious denominations into meaningful geographic associations with one another. Once we have determined the extent of such relationships and their statistical strengths, we can then venture an interpretation of the underlying forces that produce them.

There are, however, important differences between Shortridge's use of cluster techniques and the factor analytic techniques used here. As already seen, Shortridge assigned various dichotomous meanings to denominational labels. For instance, his cluster analysis involved a prejudgment that denominations A, B, and C are highly related because it is assumed that they are theologically liberal rather than conservative. In the present case as in Shortridge's work, counties serve as the units of observation. However, we shall treat religious denominations as the variables whose value, i.e. number of adherents, varies from county unit to county unit. The factor analysis is

TABLE 8

Factor-Generated Denominational Groupings

1952	FACTOR LOADING	1971	FACTOR LOADING
FACTOR GROUPING 1 (Variance = 49.3)		**FACTOR GROUPING 1** (Variance = 52.6)	
Evangelical Covenant	.78	Lutheran-Missouri Synod	.72
Baptist General Conference	.77	American Lutheran	.71
Lutheran-Missouri Synod	.72	Evangelical Covenant	.69
American Lutheran	.59	Baptist General Conference	.57
UCC/Congregational	.52	Lutheran Church in America	.56
Lutheran Church in America	.47	Catholic	.44
N.A. Baptist General Conf.	.43	UCC/Congregational	.44
FACTOR GROUPING 2 (Variance = 14.8)		**FACTOR GROUPING 2** (Variance = 14.3)	
Southern Baptist	.87	Southern Baptist	.90
Presbyterian U.S.	.81	Presbyterian U.S.	.81
Church of God (Cleveland)	.59	Church of God (Cleveland)	.64
United Methodist/Evan. N.A.	.49	United Methodist/Evan. N.A.	.64
Pentecostal Holiness	.41		
FACTOR GROUPING 3 (Variance = 12.8)		**FACTOR GROUPING 3** (Variance = 12.4)	
Church of the Nazarene	.83	Seventh-Day Adventist	.78
Intl. Foursquare Gospel	.75	Church of the Nazarene	.73
American Baptist U.S.A.	.68	American Baptist U.S.A.	.70
Free Methodist	.57	Intl. Foursquare Gospel	.72
Church of God (Anderson)	.55	Free Methodist	.60
United Presbyterian U.S.A.	.51	Baptist General Conference	.55
United Methodist/Evan. N.A.	.47	United Presbyterian U.S.A.	.50
Seventh-Day Adventist	.44	Church of God (Anderson)	.48
		Friends	.40
FACTOR GROUPING 4 (Variance = 9.1)		**FACTOR GROUPING 4** (Variance = 6.9)	
Catholic	.84	Episcopal	.76
Episcopal	.77	Catholic	.75
United Presbyterian U.S.A.	.52	Unitarian Universalist	.64
Jewish	.52	UCC/Congregational	.59
American Baptist U.S.A.	.48	American Baptist U.S.A.	.53
UCC/Congregational	.45	Jewish	.50
Lutheran Church in America	.44	United Presbyterian U.S.A.	.44
United Methodist	.41		
FACTOR GROUPING 5 (Variance = 7.5)		**FACTOR GROUPING 5** (Variance = 8.3)	
Mennonite	.78	Mennonite	.79
Brethren in Christ	.70	Evangelical Covenant	.74
Evangelical Congregational	.66	Brethren in Christ	.66
Church of the Brethren	.59	Church of the Brethren	.65
Lutheran Church in America	.48	Lutheran Church in America	.44
FACTOR GROUPING 6 (Variance = 6.5)		**FACTOR GROUPING 6** (Variance = 5.6)	
Christian Reformed	.80	Christian Reformed	.83
Reformed	.75	Reformed	.85

NOTE: Four different factor analyses were done. Both the PA 1 (principle components) and PA 2 (with iteration) options in the SPSS program manual (Nie 1975) were employed for both Varimax (Orthogonal) and Oblique rotations. The two types of rotations produced different orderings of the factors. However within each type of rotation the factors remained stable. Most importantly, the composition of the factors (i.e. denominations within them) did not change significantly across the four analyses. This table presents the results of the PA 2 Varimax procedure. The latter are most consistent with, and amenable to interpretation in terms of, patterns reported in Halvorson and Newman (1978b).

employed to determine whether denominational adherence statistics are associated across county units according to underlying elements by which denominations may be grouped. Additionally, there must be no prejudgment about how many factor groupings will emerge.

For those familiar with such techniques, these briefly are the technical details of what has been done. Using the SPSS library procedures (Nie 1975), raw statistics for the number of adherents per county per denomination were entered into a principal components analysis. Since no denominations are present in all counties (see Table 1), all missing values were defined as zero cases, thus permitting all counties to be included in the analysis of all denominational distributions. Following conventional practices, the raw factors from the principal components analysis were entered into a varimax rotation as provided in the SPSS library program. As shown in Table 8, this procedure has been performed for both the 1952 and 1971 data. The table displays the factor loadings for each denomination within its factor group, and the relative percent of explained variance accounted for by that factor. Together these six factors explain 54.4 percent of the variance in the 1952 data, and 59.2 percent of the variance in the 1971 data. Three conventional criteria have been used in generating and interpreting these six factor groupings. First, only those factors having an eigen value of at least 1 have been accepted. Second, denominations with factor loadings of .6 or greater were interpreted as strongly associated with their factors. Third, .4 has been accepted as a bottom threshold for loadings of denominations of secondary importance to their factor groupings (Rummel 1970).

Before examining the individual factor groups, there are several general features of these factors that warrant discussion. As all previous analyses of these data have shown (Shortridge 1976, 1977, Halvorson and Newman 1978b), there is remarkable stability in the relative distributions of these denominations between 1952 and 1971. The factor groups demonstrate this as clearly as did the less complex statistical and cartographic displays examined in Chapter 2. The internal compositions of these six factor groupings, the number of factors produced, and the relative variance explained by them exhibit little change. There is a slight shift between 1952 and 1971 in the variances explained by Factors 4 and 5 with the result that they switch relative position. However, both of these factors explain relatively little variance in the overall data sets. The most interesting changes pertain to shifts in the relative positions of denominations *within* their factors. These will be addressed as the individual factors are examined.

Another general characteristic of these factors is that not all the denominations in the data set (Table 1) are included in them. The Wisconsin Lutherans, the Moravians, the Seventh Day Baptists, and the Mormons are all absent. Also, the Pentecostal Holiness Church, and the North American Baptist General Conference are only present in 1952. These cases are explained by two related aspects of the geographic distributions of denominational memberships, relative size and relative density. Some extremely small denominations exhibit a high degree of geographic concentration, yet fail to be either numeric or cultural forces within their own geographic space. Six of the seven denominations just mentioned do, in fact, exhibit this type of pattern. The Wisconsin Lutherans, the Moravians, the North American Baptists, and the Seventh-Day Baptists exhibit strong geographic concentration and range in size from slightly over 6,000 to less than 400,000. The Pentecostal Holiness Church, numbering less than 100,000, is distributed in two highly concentrated areas reflecting the separate denominational groups that were merged to form the denomination. Finally, the Mormons illustrate the case of an extremely high degree of concentration combined with relatively large numeric strength. With over 2,000,000 adherents in the western states alone, the Mormons are one of the largest Protestant denominations, yet a disproportionate part of that membership is located in a relatively small historic core area. If we had disregarded the conventionally used statistical criterion of accepting only those factors with eigen values of 1., the Mormons probably would have constituted a single denominational factor accounting for extremely little overall explained variance. However, unlike the previous, more deductive typologies of Zelinsky (1961) and Shortridge (1976), the factor-generated typology presented here does not identify the Mormons as part of a nationally significant denominational factor.

These two kinds of cases underscore an important difference between the typology of groups provided here and those of Zelinsky (1961) and Sopher (1967). Both of the latter visually examine the places where either denominations or denominational families have their strongest densities, and accordingly identify these as regionally associated patterns. As we have just seen, the regional or subregional concentration of a denomination's adherents does not ensure that it will make a cultural or numerical impact on a geographical area, or that it will be statistically or culturally associated with other denominations occupying similar turf. Typologies based on deductive visual impressions of denominational data simply do not reflect these empirical complexities. It is precisely these complex statistical associations between denominational distributions that necessitate precise measurement and testing.

The most important general feature of these six factor groupings is that they do not conform in any simple way to the religio-culture regions suggested by Zelinsky (1961), the denominational pockets and regions mapped by Sopher (1967), or the regional entities created by Shortridge's (1977) Protestant-Catholic and liberal-conservative dichotomies. In fact, these six statistically significant groupings are very different from one another. As will be seen, Factors 1, 3, and 4 are broadly based national groupings of denominations that reflect a variety of historic, theological, and ethnic distinctions. They also reflect midwestern, eastern, and western geographic orientations. Only Factor 2 can easily be conceptualized as a *traditional* culture region, the South, but some strong qualifications must be added to that claim. Finally, Factors 5 and 6 represent assorted pockets of theological and ethnic distinctiveness. In Chapter 4, detailed cartographic and statistical evidence will be presented bearing on the degree of regionalism in these data. Let us first examine each factor grouping and assess the degree to which we have arrived at a meaningful typology.

Factor 1, which accounts for roughly half the explained variance in both time periods, is northern European and especially Germanic in its ethnic composition. Theologically it represents the major immigrant, continental Reformation Churches, both Lutheran and Calvinist. While Factor 1 has its center of gravity in the Midwest, its coverage is nationwide, although least prevalent in the Old South. The important point is that behind these several denominational labels there is both ethnic and theological commonality. The ALC, LCA, and Missouri Lutherans are the largest and more geographically diffuse wings of American Lutheranism. The word evangelical, of course, denotes Lutheranism. Both the Evangelical Covenant Church and a major segment of the United Church of Christ (i.e. that part formerly the Evangelical Synod of North America) are theologically Lutheran. The immigrant Calvinist tradition is also represented by the United Church of Christ (that part formerly the Reformed Church in America) and by the two immigrant Baptist (i.e. Calvinist) denominations.

The ethnic consistency of these denominations is equally strong. The ALC merger in 1960 brought together previously German, Norwegian, and Danish denominations. The LCA merger in 1962 consolidated Finnish and Danish Lutherans. The Missouri Synod was created by merging German Evangelical churches in the various American states. The Evangelical Covenant Church is a Swedish Lutheran denomination. Both the Baptist General Conference and the North American Baptist General Conference have immigrant Calvinist (i.e. Reformed) origins. The former is Swedish and the latter is German. The 1961 merger creating the United Church of Christ eclipsed an earlier merger between the Reformed Church in the United States and the Evangelical Synod of North America. Both denominations were essentially German. Moreover, during the 19th century many German immigrants outside of New England adopted Congregationalism, which is the other major group in the United Church of Christ.

Between 1952 and 1971 this important grouping of immigrant continental Protestant denominations exhibited several interesting internal changes. First, Catholics entered the listing of secondarily related denominations. Even if one speculates that many of these are German Catholics, a questionable assumption, this change still signals the beginning of significant theological diversity within this grouping. The shifts among the Protestant groups are less dramatic and can easily be understood not in terms of denominational growth *rates*, but rather in terms of the

absolute numbers involved in denominational growth patterns. The ALC and Missouri Lutherans both grew by about three-quarters of a million adherents. becoming the primary denominations in the factor. The weaker loading of the LCA reflects the fact that it fills a geographic niche in certain northeastern states in which both the Missouri Synod and the ALC are not as strongly represented. Both the North American Baptists, which dropped from the factor in 1971, and the United Church of Christ exhibited no significant geographic shifts and only modest absolute numerical growth.

Perhaps the most important thing about this factor is that none of the criteria for regional analysis employed by previous researchers would have identified this major theologically and ethnically consistent grouping of American denominations. The underlying ethnic relationships would be completely missed by Sopher's (1967) denominational pockets. Zelinsky's (1961) cultural regions are obviously too geographically narrow to produce this assortment of denominations. Factor 1 encompasses the traditional culture regions of New England, the north Atlantic states, both the upper and lower Midwest and substantial parts of the Northwest. Moreover, while Factor 1 includes one of Zelinsky's denominational families— all but one Lutheran group is included—the inclusion of Baptists, the United Church of Christ, and in 1971, Catholics, demonstrates the limitations of that approach. The emergence of Catholics in this group would not be detected by Shortridge's Protestant—Catholic dichotomy, and the conservative—liberal dichotomy used by both Shortridge (1976, 1977) and Kelley (1972) completely obliterates the ethnic and theological unity of this grouping. Thus, while Factor 1 does not conform to any of these previous approaches or the criteria by which they are created, it does exhibit stability across both time periods, and is amenable to meaningful interpretation and explanation according to salient theological, ethnic, and therefore historic patterns.

Factor 2 is the only factor grouping among the six that strongly resembles a *traditional* geographic religio-culture region. With a few minor exceptions, this is essentially the same set of denominations that Zelinsky (1961) identified as a "southern" regional group encompassing both the five states of the Old South and parts of the southwestern states as well. It exhibits impressive consistency in terms of both the relative variance explained by the factor, just under 15 percent, and the internal positions of its denominations. As noted earlier the Pentecostal Holiness Church dropped from this factor in 1971. The remaining four denominations appear in the same relative order, and by 1971, they all exhibit strongly associated factor loadings (all above .6).

The ethnic and theological unity of this group requires little elaboration. The Presbyterians, the Baptists, and the Methodists all originated from Calvinist reform movements within the Anglican Church. In this case, the

Southern Presbyterians represent colonial period settlers from the British Isles. Southern Presbyterians have remained more theologically conservative than the other major American Presbyterian bodies, and organizationally separate from them as well. The Southern Baptists and the United Methodists are, of course, the two largest Anglo-Calvinist denominations in the United States. The Churches of God are a major 19th century native American extension of the Baptist tradition, again following conservative Calvinist theology. The Pentecostal Holiness Church was created by mergers between several small Baptist and Methodist groups, and adheres to Methodist polity and theology. The so-called "southern" group then, is ethnically Anglo-American. All of the denominations in this factor trace their theological origins and present-day beliefs to the several wings of the English Reformation, the Calvinist reaction against the Anglican or Episcopal Church. Although substantively different from Factor 1, Factor 2 exhibits similarly homogeneous ethnic and theological characteristics.

There are several complex features of this set of denominations. It is true that each of these denominations exhibits its strongest concentrations in the southern and southwestern states. However, the Southern Baptists and the United Methodists are the two largest American Protestant denominations, each of them being more than four times larger than the next largest Protestant group (see Table 1). Moreover, the Southern Baptists and the United Methodists are both truly national in scope, being represented in 1971 in 72 percent and 96 percent respectively of all counties. Simply stated, while the center of gravity of this factor is undeniably southern and southwestern, the two largest groups in the factor can be found in some strength in almost every state of the union. That places an important qualification upon calling this factor "southern," and viewing it as a geographically distinct regional entity.

In that context, the increased statistical associations in this factor between 1952 and 1971 are rather unexpected. The United Methodists not only increased their statistical association with this factor, but also dropped out of Factor 4. These statistical patterns suggest increasing social homogeneity within the factor, and represent a distinct counter-trend to what already has been seen in Factor 1. In fact, the assertion of Hill (1967) and others that the American South is becoming more culturally diverse owing to the immigration of Catholics, Episcopalians, and other Protestant groups is not supported in these data. These comments, of course, point to the issue of increasing and decreasing levels of religious and cultural pluralism during the 1952-1971 period. One must also consider the extent to which any measure of religion can accurately serve as an indicator of cultural stability or change. These matters are discussed later (the focus of Chapter 5). Setting aside these kinds of issues for the moment, if it is admitted that this factor is at least centered in the southern and south-

western states, its increased statistical coherence also contradicts Shortridge's claim (1977) that the Bible Belt is diminishing. In summary, what at first appears to be a geographically regional factor is actually not precisely that. Yet, to the extent that this factor exhibits a regional orientation, its statistical trends contradict previously claimed patterns of decreasing religio-cultural distinctiveness in this part of the nation.

Factor 3 accounts for just under 13 percent of the explained variance in both time periods. It contains all of the nationally based, non-southern wings of the Presbyterian, native American Baptist, and Methodist traditions. Stated in other terms, these are primarily Anglo-Calvinist denominations that are widely distributed in all parts of the nation except the South. As has been seen already, the southern oriented branches of these traditions are all contained in Factor 2. The presence of the Church of the Nazarene, the Seventh-Day Adventists, and the Foursquare Gospel Church gives this factor a central Great Plains and western orientation.

The ethnic consistency of the factor is mildly diminished in 1971 with the entrance of the Baptist General Conference, essentially a Swedish immigrant denomination. All of the other denominations in the factor, like those in its more southern counterpart, are American branches of the dissent from Anglicanism. The United Presbyterians and the American Baptists are both the products of nationwide mergers within traditional families. It has been noted that the United Methodists dropped from this factor in 1971. However, both the Free Methodists and a rapidly growing Methodist denomination, the Church of the Nazarene, are present in both time periods. In addition to the American Baptists, the Baptist faith is represented by the Seventh-Day Adventists, the Church of God (Anderson), and the Foursquare Gospel Church. In spite of the diversity of denominational labels, eight of the ten denominations in this factor between 1952 and 1971 are theologically either Baptist, Methodist, or Presbyterian. The Friends, while also derived from the British rather than the continental Reformation, do represent a somewhat different theological emphasis. Thus only two denominations, the Friends and the Baptist General Conference, both appearing for the first time in 1971, indicate theological and ethnic diversity respectively. In other words, much like Factor 1, this is a nationally distributed grouping with unquestionable ethnic and theological consistency, for which the 1971 data show some increases in diversity or pluralism.

There are several other interesting characteristics of this denominational grouping. More than any other factor, this one can legitimately be viewed as the major representative of evangelical Protestantism. It contains the major 19th century extensions of Baptism and Methodism, products of the second great awakening and the holiness movement. The dramatic shift in the relative position of the Seventh Day Adventists, and the ability of the Church of the Nazarene to hold its relative position within this factor confirm our earlier impressions (Halvorson and Newman 1978b) that both denominations are in the process of attaining national stature. As with the denominational groupings in the other factors, previously employed criteria for classifying denominations would not identify this theologically and ethnically consistent set.

Factor 4 is the last of the three major nationally based groupings. Between 1952 and 1971 the percent of variance explained by this factor decreased, as did the strength of the factor loadings for the two primary denominations within it, Catholics and Episcopalians. Throughout the period this remains the most ethnically and theologically diverse of the six factor groupings. It also exhibits a variety of internal shifts. Although this is a national grouping, the presence in 1971 of Episcopalians, Unitarian Universalists, Catholics, and Jews clearly shows the northeastern, metropolitan orientation of this factor. As previous analyses have shown (Halvorson and Newman 1978b; Newman and Halvorson 1979), the last two groupings have their strongest densities in the northeastern population corridor and in metropolitan locations outside of that broadly defined geographic area. Moreover, in 1952 there were five denominations in this factor that were created through organizational mergers involving denominations with strong northeastern distributions. These "merged" denominations are the United Methodists, the Lutheran Church in America, the United Church of Christ, the United Presbyterian Church, and the American Baptist Churches. In 1952 all five of these groups are of secondary statistical importance to this factor (factor loadings below .6) and exhibit similar statistical association with at least one other factor. While two of these denominations, the Methodists and the Lutherans, drop from the factor in 1971, the Unitarian-Universalists are added in that year. Interestingly, they too are a merged denomination with adherents through the nation, but with a strong traditional denominational emphasis in the Northeast. While for the moment we have focused upon the geographic orientation of this factor, it, like the others, is best understood in terms of ethnic characteristics and historic patterns of immigration.

The denominations in Factor 4 reflect two very different, but equally influential periods in American immigration history. The Protestant denominations are the remnants of America's colonial religions and are mainly, though not exclusively, drawn from the British Isles. The Catholics and Jews derive in large part from the two waves of the Great Migration (Jones 1960) that was curtailed by the 1924 National Origins Quota Act. Additionally, it should be noted that German Jews are also a colonial period group, and that the Catholic trends must also be understood in terms of more recent Spanish-speaking immigrants.

Turning first to the Protestant denominations, the Episcopalians (Anglicans), the United Presbyterians (originally Scotch-Irish Convenanters), the United Methodists (from the Oxford Movement), the United Church of Christ (formerly Separatists, Puritans, and later Congregationalist), the Unitarians (a reform movement from within Congregationalism) and the American Baptist (followers of Roger Williams in Rhode Island) are all Anglo-American denominations that were established here prior to the American Revolution. While American cultural traditions emphasize Anglo dominance in the colonial period, a number of continental Protestant denominations were also well established. The American Lutheran Church, which dropped from the factor in 1971, is the oldest branch of American Lutheranism, originating with German, Dutch, and Scandinavian immigrants in the early 1600s. Other German Protestant immigrants during this period formed the Evangelical Synod of North America and the Reformed Church in the United States, both of which are now contained within the United Church of Christ. Viewed in this perspective, the Protestant denominations in Factor 4 exhibit theological and even ethnic diversity, but remarkable historical continuity. Two types of Protestant denominations are conspicuously absent from this factor. They are the other major branches of the continental Reformation churches and the nativist, evangelical Baptist and Methodist denominations. These, of course, are concentrated in Factors 1 and 3 respectively.

When viewed in terms of its ethnic diversity, the American Jewish community encompasses both the colonial immigration and the Great Migration. Substantial numbers of German Jews immigrated along with their Protestant counterparts well before the American Revolution. Eastern European Jews immigrated in large numbers at the turn of the last century. While it can also accurately be argued that Catholics are a colonial period denomination (consider the French, Spanish, and Italian explorers, Mexican-Americans, and of course, the founding of Maryland), the Great Migration contained substantial numbers of Irish, Italian, and other ethnic Catholics. More recent 20th century Spanish-speaking immigrants have added to the internal ethnic diversity of this denomination. Factor 4 then is the "transmuting pot" (Herberg, 1955) of Anglo, and to a lesser degree German, Protestants and ethnically diverse Catholics and Jews who have long represented the theological and social pluralism of the entire northeastern part of the nation.

The internal dynamics within the factor between 1952 and 1971 mirror some important historical as well as recent national trends. Catholics exhibit a diminished statistical association with the factor in 1971, falling just behind Episcopalians in relative position. While Catholic adherence grew by 51 percent during this period, Catholics also became more evenly dispersed throughout the nation. By 1971 Catholics were present in 92 percent of all counties, an increase of 261 counties since 1952 (see Table 1). The reduced factor loading is less an indication that Catholics became a weaker denomination in this factor than a reflection of their changed relative national distribution. A similar process is reflected in the diminished factor loading for the United Presbyterians. In this case, an organizational merger with a heavily midwestern branch of Presbyterianism (the former Presbyterian Church in North America) explains the statistical indication of geographic diffusion. The continued presence in Factors 3 and 4 of the United Presbyterians and the American Baptists during both time periods reflects long term historic extensions of these two colonial Anglo-Protestant traditions into the middle section of the country in the form of "new light" Presbyterianism and nativist, evangelical Baptist denominations. The mergers through which these two denominations were formed were really reunions. Similarly, the continued presence in Factors 1 and 4 of the United Church (especially its Reformed and Evangelical branches) and the Catholic Church reflects historic excursions of continental Europeans into the American heartland.

In summary, Factor 4 cannot be understood in terms of similarities in denominational names or narrowly defined geographic regions. Between 1952 and 1971 this factor encompasses America's so-called "three religion pluralism," as well as every major Protestant family name. However, this diversity consistently reflects two great periods of American immigration. Geographically these denominations span the traditional culture regions of New England, the northern and mid-Atlantic states, and the upper and lower Midwest. While there is a distinct northeastern orientation, this grouping is national in scope.

Factor 5 more resembles a geographically discrete religio-culture region than any of the other factor groupings. However, neither Zelinsky (1961), Sopher (1967), nor Shortridge (1976, 1977) identify this particular regional entity. These denominations are essentially Pennsylvanian and German. In fact, there are only two significant exceptions to that characterization. In 1962 the United Lutheran Church, a Germanic denomination, merged with several Scandinavian groups to become the Lutheran Church in America, that merger creating both ethnic and geographic diversity. The Evangelical Covenant Church, although much smaller, mirrors the LCA distribution, extending into parts of New England, the upper Midwest, the Northwest and the West Coast. The result is a group of primarily German denominations having a strong and limited geographic core area in Pennsylvania and adjacent states, but that exhibit definite geographic strength in different regions of the nation outside that core area.

The primary group in this factor is the Mennonites. These are German Anabaptists (re-baptizers) who fled Europe in the late 1600s, finding religious toleration in the colonies only in Pennsylvania. The two Brethren denominations in this factor resulted from a schism. The Brethren groups also are dissenting German Baptists, in this case pietists, who immigrated in the early 1700s. The

Evangelical Congregational Church, like the Lutheran Church in America, consists of German Lutherans. The former dissented from the 1922 merger that created the United Evangelical Church. The Evangelical Covenant Church is a Swedish immigrant church also following the pietist interpretation of the Baptist tradition. Simply stated, Factor 5 represents the German and Swedish, theologically conservative Baptist and Lutheran traditions. The mainstream of these religio-ethnic traditions is located in Factor 1. As will next be seen, the conservative Calvinist branch of Factor 1 is represented by Factor 6.

Factor 6, consisting of the Christian Reformed Church and the Reformed Church in America, represents a theologically conservative branch of Presbyterianism (Calvinist) and is ethnically Dutch. They are the only colonial period immigrants not heavily represented in Factor 4. These two denominations separated from each other only in the 1830s, and, while they remain organizationally separate, in the larger national religious context they are still theologically and ethnically one entity. Factor 6 does not represent a discrete geographic region. Rather, as individual denominational maps indicate (Halvorson and Newman 1978b), this factor consists of certain pockets of strength in parts of upper New York State, Illinois, Michigan, and one corner of Pennsylvania. It is not surprising that these two denominations, with a combined adherence of barely half a million people, provide very little explained variance in the overall data sets. These pockets of Dutch Presbyterians obviously contribute a strong religio-ethnic flavor to a small number of a small geographic areas. Again, historic patterns of ethnic and theological distinctiveness that do not fit previous "regional" typologies explain the emergence of this factor.

In summary, this chapter has focused upon the need for some form of typology permitting examination of data at a level beyond that of individual denominations. Through factor analytic techniques, the proposition that there are clear statistical relationships among certain of the 35 denominations has been verified. Setting aside temporarily the question of the degree of regionalization of these groupings, this chapter has focused upon the historical, ethnic, and theological continuities within the six denominational groups or types. Two of these groups, nominally reflecting the north and south Atlantic regions, show strong Anglo-Calvinist composition. They understandably represent the colonial heritage of these two sections of the nation. Moreover, the northern group also reflects the Catholic and Jewish immigrations of the last century and a half. A third major grouping, provisionally identified as midwestern, is dominated by continental Protestants rather than those from the British Isles. It is of little surprise that the several major branches of Lutheranism represent the prevailing cultural and theological mode here. The fourth national grouping of denominations clearly consists of frontier, often native American denominations.

These are primarily 19th century reforms of Baptism and Methodism, and are obviously western in orientation. The remaining two denominational groups, German pietists centered in Pennsylvania and the Ohio Valley, and two clusters of Dutch Reformed Calvinists, are not considered to be of national significance and require little further analysis. Rather, they are religio-cultural pockets with very little geographic depth.

Our concern in this chapter has been to explain the historical, ethnic, and theological meanings of these group-ings, and to determine that they are, in fact, much more than statistical accidents. The regional hypothesis has been touched upon only slightly in this chapter for two reasons. First, it was premature to address that issue before clearly establishing both the fact and nature of this new typology. Second, the question of regionalization is sufficiently important and complex as to require separate and comprehensive treatment. Accordingly, Chapter 4 next provides a detailed analysis of the major religious regions of the United States.

4

The Major Religious Regions

MEASURING THE REGIONAL COMPONENT

The preceding chapter has presented a new typology of religious denominations. At the outset it was noted that the question of typology and that of religious regionalism are, in fact, the same. However, Chapter 3 has not focused upon the regional aspects of the typology. While regional orientations are very obviously present in the six types of religious groupings, primary consideration has been given to the historic, ethnic, and theological continuities within the types. In other words, before exploring the utility of the typology for regional analyses, it was first necessary to demonstrate the meaningfulness of these types. They are much more than just statistical entities. Rather, these statistical associations exist because of underlying social and historical connections between these several sets of denominations.

Having established that the typology does make sense, the degree to which these types of denominational groups are geographically regional may now be examined. Three themes about religious regionalism are developed in this chapter. First, as depicted by this typology, American religion is unquestionably regional in nature. Each type of denominational grouping occupies a rather broad geographical space (or set of spaces) in which other types are not strongly represented. These areas of relatively exclusive strength fit together in a jigsaw-like pattern. Second, there also are large numbers of counties in the nation in which these different denominational groupings coexist with one another. Said differently, these regional types do not entirely occupy mutually exclusive spaces. While these data yield regional patterns, the term "regional" must be used with care and with qualifications. Third, these regional

patterns exhibit some important similarities to and differences from previously proposed typologies. In a variety of ways the assertions of Zelinsky (1961), Sopher (1967), and Shortridge (1976, 1977) are alternately supported and refuted. Both cartographic and statistical evidence support these three themes. Let us first examine cartographic indications of the fact and extent of religious regions.

A series of maps have been created with which the extent and precise locations of the religious regions in these data may be viewed. Since thus far the various ways in which these data have been measured indicate more stability than change during the 1952-1971 period, only the more recent 1971 data have been mapped here. Shifts in the denominational compositions of the six types for the period have, of course, already been discussed in the preceding chapter. Additionally, only the four major types are treated here. Both the Dutch Presbyterian and German Pietist types (i.e., groups 5 and 6) are sufficiently small in numbers of adherents and geographic coverage to make further analysis of them redundant. They are essentially religio-ethnic pockets of strength that depart from the national patterns created by the first four types of denominational groupings.

The four maps discussed here were created by the following procedures. The typology itself was, of course, produced by the factor analytic techniques previously discussed. A statistic called a factor score (Rummel 1970), indicating the relative strength of each type in each county, was created. These factor scores were then converted into standard scores that could be categorized according to their means, and standard deviations from those means. For each type, those counties with standard scores more than one standard deviation above the mean were defined as high strength counties. This category typically accounts for between 100 and 200 county units and is given the darkest shading on each of the four maps. Counties falling within

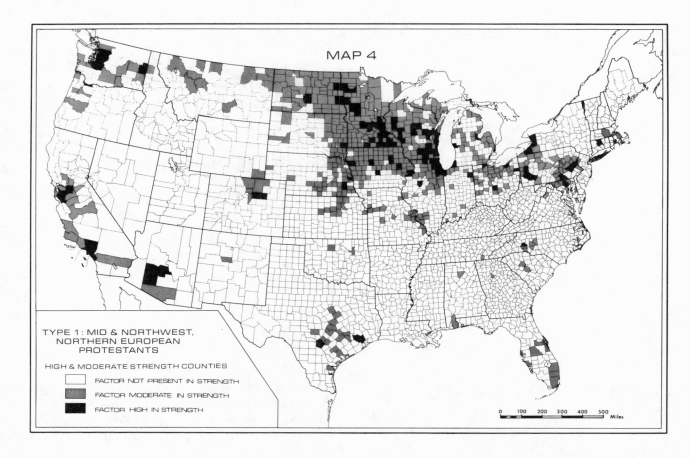

MAP 4

TYPE 1: MID & NORTHWEST,
NORTHERN EUROPEAN
PROTESTANTS

HIGH & MODERATE STRENGTH COUNTIES

- FACTOR NOT PRESENT IN STRENGTH
- FACTOR MODERATE IN STRENGTH
- FACTOR HIGH IN STRENGTH

0   100   200   300   400   500
Miles

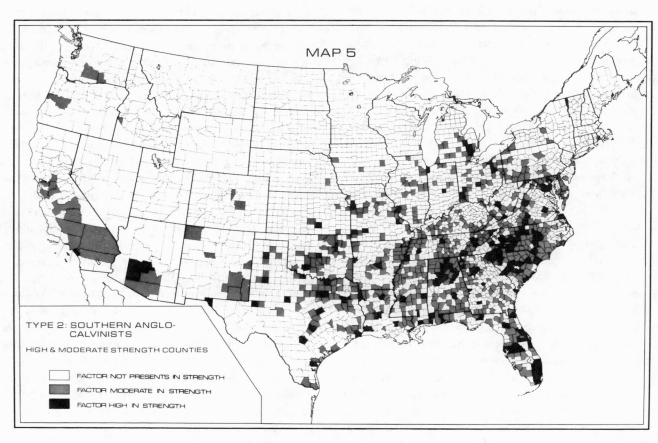

MAP 5

TYPE 2: SOUTHERN ANGLO-
CALVINISTS

HIGH & MODERATE STRENGTH COUNTIES

- FACTOR NOT PRESENTS IN STRENGTH
- FACTOR MODERATE IN STRENGTH
- FACTOR HIGH IN STRENGTH

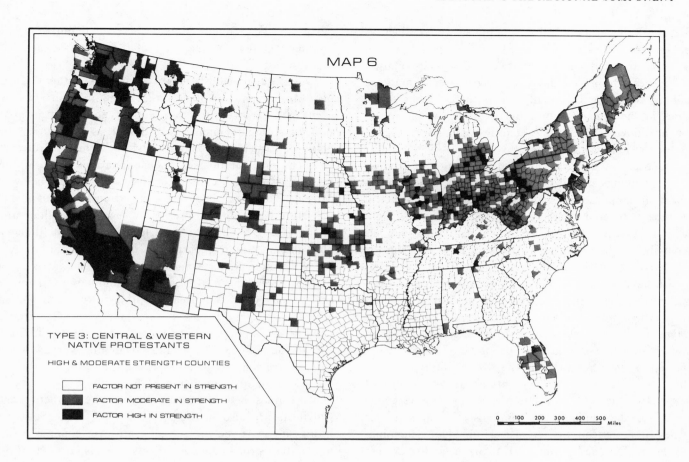

MAP 6

TYPE 3: CENTRAL & WESTERN
NATIVE PROTESTANTS

HIGH & MODERATE STRENGTH COUNTIES

- [ ] FACTOR NOT PRESENT IN STRENGTH
- [ ] FACTOR MODERATE IN STRENGTH
- [ ] FACTOR HIGH IN STRENGTH

0 100 200 300 400 500
Miles

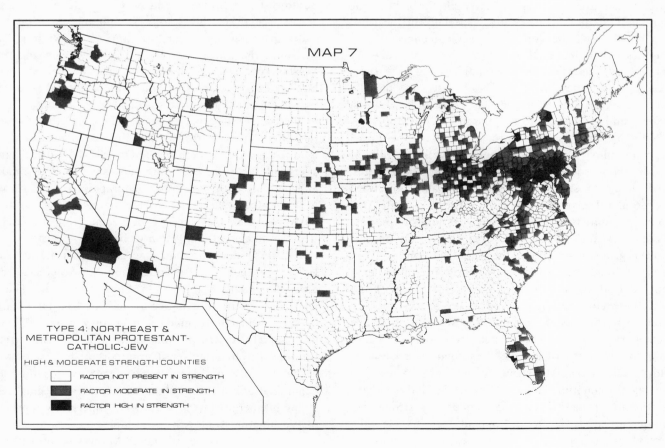

MAP 7

TYPE 4: NORTHEAST &
METROPOLITAN PROTESTANT-
CATHOLIC-JEW

HIGH & MODERATE STRENGTH COUNTIES

- [ ] FACTOR NOT PRESENT IN STRENGTH
- [ ] FACTOR MODERATE IN STRENGTH
- [ ] FACTOR HIGH IN STRENGTH

one standard deviation but above the mean were defined as moderate strength counties for each of the types. For each map there are usually between 500 and 600 such counties, and they bear the next lightest shading. On each map the remaining county units, usually about three-fourths of all counties in the United States, fall at or below the mean. These are obviously "weak" counties for the respective types and are left unshaded.

Two aspects of these methods of mapping the denominational groupings should be noted. First, the shaded areas on the four maps do *not* indicate all counties in which a given type is located. Rather, the two shaded areas highlight those places where a denominational grouping has either high or moderate density. Second, by converting the raw data to standard scores, means, and standard deviations, we have, in effect, combined within the lowest category (i.e., the unshaded areas) on each map those counties where a type is weak and a small number of counties where that type simply does not appear. In other words, the maps do not convey the fact that most denominational groupings are present in most but not all of the 3073 counties.

The first grouping, Type 1, contains denominations of primarily Continental Reformation theology and Germanic ethnicity. Understandably, it contains all three major branches of American Lutheranism. Individual denominational maps for these groups (Halvorson and Newman 1978b) indicate areas of primary strength throughout the northern half of the United States, especially in the Midwest. Map 4 shows the composite regional concentration for this first denominational grouping. The upper category consists of 114 counties. While relatively few of these high category counties are in the Northeast, they literally encircle the American Midwest. They begin in Buffalo, and extend both southward to Pittsburgh and west to Cleveland. This band of regional strength borders the Great Lakes, continuing through Michigan, northern Illinois, Wisconsin, Minnesota, and into the northern Plains states. Isolated areas of strength in the West and Southwest appear around Denver, Phoenix, San Diego, Seattle, and Spokane. A somewhat unique concentration of German Lutherans in Texas (Jordan, 1969) marks the only appearance of this group in strength in the American South.

Areas of moderate strength for this denominational grouping appear in three different kinds of places. First, most of these counties are located in the spaces between high category counties throughout the Midwest. Like the high category counties, they stretch from western Pennsylvania to the northern Plains. A second type of location for these moderately strong counties is adjacent to high category counties in both California and southern Texas. Finally, Type 1 appears in moderately strong, but discontinuous, areas in New England, central Georgia, southern Florida, and several southwestern locations. In summary, Type 1 consists largely of Germanic immigrants and their descendants, following Continental Reformation theologies, especially Lutheranism. Although present in all

parts of the United States, these denominations predominate in the northern half of the nation, especially in the Midwest.

Type 2 was previously identified as the "southern" grouping. More than any other set of denominations this one, even upon cursory inspection, appears to exhibit an exceptionally strong regional orientation. It is, of course, composed of British Isles, Anglo-Calvinist forms of Protestantism. The map for this set of denominations (Map 5) holds few surprises. High category counties are largely below the Mason-Dixon line. They are conspicuously absent in both the Northeast and Northwest. A few metropolitan areas in the Midwest, among them Cleveland, Detroit, Indianapolis, and St. Louis, depart from this pattern. Similarly, in the West, both Phoenix and Los Angeles emerge as islands of high strength for this set of denominations. However, the boundary of the area of primary strength for this regional grouping begins in Washington, D.C., stretches down the Atlantic Coast to Florida, and across the Southeast to the plains of Texas and Oklahoma. Throughout the southern region, urban areas make the strongest showing, the most pronounced being in Alabama.

Most areas of secondary strength for the southern Anglo-Calvinists are also predictably confined to the Southeast, filling in gaps between high category counties. Some moderately strong counties for this type also extend into the Southwest and Midwest, and provide some islands of moderate strength in the Southwest and on the West Coast. More precisely such counties appear in western Texas, Missouri, the Chicago area, Central Michigan, and around Washington, D.C. Such counties also appear adjacent to high category counties in both California and Arizona, as well as in isolated locations near Denver, Albuquerque, and in the San Francisco Bay area. While there is no question that this is a southern grouping, it is equally clear that the unique national strength of the United Methodist Church is a crucial factor in extending this type, in both moderate and high strength, into other geographic regions. However, to the extent that regional labels are justified, and obviously we feel they are, Type 2 may appropriately be understood as southern Anglo-Calvinist.

The third denominational set is also primarily Anglo-Protestant, but is best understood as America's second generation, rather than "old line" Churches. The predominant groups are native American frontier Churches, most of which have nineteenth century origins. They are the uniquely American modifications of Baptism, Methodism, and Presbyterianism. The important feature of Map 6 is the absence of high category counties for this set of denominations in the older southeastern region. Some strength emerges in the area from upper New York State to Washington, D.C. A band of high category counties then runs westward through the lower Midwest, scattered across Ohio and Indiana, and into the central Great Plains. However, the blanket of high category counties in both the West Coast and northwestern areas leave little question about the regional orientation of this type.

Counties indicating moderate strength follow the pattern of high category counties, and again predominate in the western section of the nation. This category adds some new strength in central Michigan to an already established pattern that stretches from upper New York State and Delaware, through Ohio, Indiana, and Illinois. Additional counties in Kansas and Nebraska complete the pattern. Type 3 may best be understood as primarily western, native American Calvinists. This characterization is qualified only by the entrance of the Friends into this denominational grouping in 1971.

Type 4 represents an important departure from the kind of ethnic and theological homogeneity of the previous three types. Two sizeable minority religious communities, Jews and Roman Catholics, are both strongly associated with this grouping. Catholics, of course, constitute nearly half of the reported religious adherence in both time periods. The American Jewish population is nearly twice the size of most major Protestant groups, excepting only the United Methodist Church and the Southern Baptist Convention. The remaining denominations in this set are the northern analogue to the southern Anglo-Calvinists. These are "old line" British Isles, colonial Protestant groups. Together these theologically diverse communions comprise what Kennedy (1944, 1952) and subsequently others have called the "triple melting pot." They are the core of what Herberg (1955) has called America's "three-religion pluralism"—three very different theological communities living side by side and, to a degree at least, tolerating each others' differences. As our popular images of these groups would suggest, Type 4 is clearly northeastern and especially metropolitan in character. These features of Type 4 are clearly delineated on Map 7.

Counties in the highest category are most numerous in the northeastern quadrant of the nation, especially in the population corridor known as "Megalopolis." This includes much of Pennsylvania, New York, New Jersey, and the New England states. High category counties also extend into the American Midwest. Virtually every major metropolitan area between Buffalo and Chicago, Pittsburgh and Cincinnati, is included. Isolated areas of primary strength also appear in southern Florida, Louisiana, several locations in Texas, and in the San Francisco Bay area.

As with the other three major types, counties of secondary strength are typically located adjacent to those of primary strength. As would be expected, such counties are strongly clustered in the northeastern part of the nation. They begin to thin in the Midwest and disappear entirely in the Great Plains states. A very weak scattering of these counties appears across the southern states. There are but two exceptions to that pattern. Louisiana makes a strong showing because of the presence of French Catholics (Cajuns), and there is a strong showing of Mexican-American Catholics along the southwestern border. Metropolitan areas in New Mexico and southern California exhibit addi-

tional counties of secondary strength, but they are far less prevalent in the northwestern states. Thus, although some significant outliers exist in the South and Southwest, there seems to be little need to qualify the assertion that this "three religion pluralism" of Catholics, Jews, and "old line" Anglo-Protestants is essentially a northeastern and metropolitan phenomena.

These counties of moderate strength indicate another important difference between Type 4 and the other three major national groupings. Type 4 exhibits far fewer counties of moderate strength than any of the other three national groupings (378 counties as compared to 539, 614, and 612 respectively). It seems probable that what we have previously observed for the distribution of American Jews (Newman and Halvorson 1979) is true for this entire cluster of denominations as well. Specifically, large numbers of adherents are located in a relatively small number of counties. In other words, there are fewer counties of secondary strength because the adherents for this set of denominations are less evenly distributed across the counties in which they are located. Accordingly, Type 4, more than the other types, has many more counties falling near to but below the mean and thus appearing in the unshaded area on Map 7.

Let us summarize the regional features depicted by these four maps. The locales within which these four major types of denominational groupings exhibit their strongest presences clearly indicate regional patterns for American religion. If one focuses not upon the total distribution patterns for the four types, but upon their areas of primary and moderate strength, a pattern of discrete territories or turfs emerges. Type 1, containing groups primarily associated with the Continental Reformation, is most strongly represented in the upper Midwest. Type 2, consisting of denominations associated with "old line" Anglo-Calvinism, is strongest in the "Old South" or south Atlantic states. Type 3, composed of frontier versions of Anglo-Calvinism, typically native American Protestants, is strongest in the lower Midwest and Far West. Type 4, representing the triple melting pot of Anglo-Protestants from the colonial northeastern states, and more recent Catholic and Jewish immigrants from the "Great Migration," is northeastern and especially metropolitan in character.

The degree to which these national groupings of denominations have partitioned the available geographic space is clearly illustrated in the one place where several of the types border upon each other, the Great Plains states. In terms of their geographic origins in the United States none of these denominational groupings really claim the Plains as a homeland. Yet, Types 1, 2, and 3 all occupy the Plains in strength. However, each occupies a different portion of this region, the northern, southern, and central areas respectively. The Great Plains then represent a jig-saw like boundary area between three of the four major groupings of denominations.

TABLE 9

**Regional, Theological, and Ethnic
Characteristics of the Six Denominational
Groupings Produced by Factor Analysis**

NO.	REGIONAL PREDOMINANCE	ETHNIC FEATURES	LEADING DENOMINATIONS
	MAJOR NATIONAL TYPES		
1	Midwest & Northwest	Germanic Scandinavian	Continental Reformation Churches: Lutheran and Evangelical
2	Southern	British Isles	Baptist, Methodist, Presbyterian
3	Central & Western	Native American	Anglo-Protestant, American branches: Adventist, Nazarene, Baptist, Presbyterian, and Methodist
4	Northeast & Metropolitan	British Isles Eastern & Southern European minority groups. Various racial minority groups	Catholic, Jewish, major branches of Anglo-Protestants: Episcopal, Methodist, United Church, Presbyterian
	SUBREGIONAL TYPES		
5		Germanic	Pietist, i.e., conservative branches of Continental Calvinist Mennonites and Brethren
6		Dutch	Continental Presbyterians—Reformed Churches

The regional, theological, and ethnic characteristics of the entire six-fold typology developed in this chapter and in Chapter 3 is summarized in Table 9. This table may usefully be compared to earlier typologies, especially those of Zelinsky (Table 6) and Shortridge (Table 7). However, before doing so, one remaining aspect of the typology developed here should be examined.

THE ANATOMY OF REGIONALISM

At various points in both this chapter and Chapter 3 we have stated that this typology supports the idea of religious regionalism in the United States, but that the concept of regionalism requires some qualification. Similarly, while we have shown that discrete turfs emerge if one examines high category counties for each type of religious grouping, we have also stated repeatedly that all four major types are present in most places in the United States. The specific question arises, how great is the extent of overlap between these four national types of religious groupings? To what degree do the ostensibly separate turfs of the four major groupings "bleed" into one another and thus blur the initial image of discrete regions? In this case, statistical indices provide an important supplement to the four maps just presented.

Tables, 10, 11, and 12 provide a variety of statistical summaries of the extent to which the four major denominational groupings exist in the same or different county units. Moreover, each of the three tables provides a different piece of information about the ways in which the four major types of denominational groups are geographically related to one another. Table 10 affords an examination of the degree of discreteness in both high and moderate strength counties for each of the four types. In each instance, the first column in Table 10 shows the total number of counties in which each religious grouping registers high strength. The second column shows the number of these counties that are "discrete," or not shared at that same level of strength by any other religious grouping. The third column reports the percentage of discrete counties for each denomination. The table provides this information for both high and moderate strength counties for the four types of denominational groupings.

TABLE 10

**Numbers of Total and Discrete Counties for the
Four Major Types of Religious Groupings**

TYPE	HIGH STRENGTH COUNTIES			MODERATE STRENGTH COUNTIES		
	Total	Discrete	Percent Discrete	Total	Discrete	Percent Discrete
1	112	78	69.6	503	334	63.0
2	159	114	71.7	607	419	69.0
3	109	65	59.6	600	280	46.7
4	121	74	61.2	374	147	39.3

NOTE: Moderate and high strength are defined as within one and above one standard deviation above the mean factor scores respectively; i.e., the same measures mapped in Maps 4 thru 7. As is explained in the text, the term "discrete" means counties that are not shared by another type of denominational grouping at the same level of strength.

The general pattern emerging from Table 10 confirms the initial visual impressions gleaned from Maps 4 through 7. Counties occupied by any of the four types in their highest degree of strength tend not to be occupied by other denominational groupings at similar levels of strength. This pattern is most pronounced for the midwestern and southern groupings, Types 1 and 2. This is indicated by 69.6 and 71.7 percent of the high category cases being discrete for these two types respectively. It is important to note that these two groupings are the most theologically different from each other, contrasting colonial period Anglo-Protestant Churches with continental Reformation Churches of more recent immigration. Similarly, these two types of denominational groupings provide the greatest amount of explained variance in the entire data set for both time periods (see Table 8). The percentages of discrete counties for Types 3 and 4 are a bit less impressive. This, however, is not surprising. Type 3 consists of the western oriented, native Protestant denominations. Some of the major groups in this set have rather wide-spread geographic distributions, especially the Church of the Nazarene and the Seventh-Day Adventists. In this sense, one might have anticipated less geographic discreteness for this set of denominations. Similarly, Type 4 contains two large denominations, Catholics and Jews, both of which exhibit strong metropolitan concentrations outside of Type 4's primary northeastern region. Again, a less tidy pattern of regionalization obtains, thus generating a lower percentage of discrete counties.

For all four types the percentage of discrete, moderate strength counties mirrors that of high strength counties. This is entirely consistent with the mapped data. On all four maps moderate strength counties create a fringe or shadow pattern around high strength counties. Since it is now clear that each of the four groupings in a sense radiates out from a regional core or central area, it is quite understandable that moderate strength counties indicate lower levels of discreteness. They gradually lapse into diffuse transitional areas where the four denominational types create different patterns of numerical parity with one another. Specific patterns of overlap are statistically summarized in Table 11. However, before examining this table one very important additional point should be stressed concerning Table 10.

TABLE 11

Moderate and High Strength Counties by the Degree of Sharing among the Four Major Types of Religious Groupings

COUNTIES SHARED AT HIGH OR MODERATE STRENGTH							
	1 Type		2 Types		3 Types		4 Types
	N	Percent	N	Percent	N	Percent	N	Percent
Total High Strength Counties N = 501	331	66.1	60	23.9	14	8.4	2	1.6
Total Moderate Strength Counties N = 2111	1180	55.9	369	34.9	51	7.2	10	1.9

NOTE: High and moderate strength for a type of religious grouping in a county are defined operationally as less than and more than one standard deviation above the mean factor score per county for each type respectively.
Percentages are generated by multiplying the number of counties by the number of types occupying such counties.

Like the four maps, Table 10 does not compare all counties in which the four types of denominational groupings are located. It only compares counties in which these four types exhibit high or moderate strength. However, as noted earlier, each type occupies a minimum of 2000 counties in addition to those enumerated in the tables. In other words, as we stated earlier, most of these four types of denominational groups exist in some strength in most of the 3073 counties in the United States. Thus, when it is shown that roughly two-thirds of high or moderate strength counties for each type are discrete at that level for the type, there is another side to that picture. Obviously, very large numbers of counties contain various degrees of mixture of the four types. Such mixtures constitute one way

in which levels of religious pluralism may be measured at the county level. That issue is the central focus of Chapter 5. For the moment our concern is to depict and understand some of the internal dynamics of and the extent of religious regionalism.

Table 11 allows a more detailed inspection of the patterns in Table 10. Specifically, Table 11 treats separately the 501 cases in which one or more regional types claims a high level of adherents, as well as the 2111 cases in which one or more of the regional types claims a moderate level of adherence. For these two sets of occurrences the table lists the number of counties in which any one, two, three, or all four denominational groupings claim a high or moderate level of adherence. In other words, this table depicts the exact extent of parity or turf sharing between religious groupings at the county level.

Turning first to the high category counties, over two-thirds of them (66.1 percent) are claimed as a high category county by only one regional type (i.e., 331 of the total 501 counties). This is the total number of discrete high category counties in the entire 1971 data set as represented by the four major groupings. This statistic is, of course, consistent with the previous cartographic and numerical data suggesting that each of the four types has a clearly delineated geographic center of gravity. Next, 23.9 percent of the cases fall within counties that are claimed as high by at least two denominational groups. These 60 counties are most probably metropolitan area counties. Perhaps the most dramatic findings in the table pertain to those counties shared by three or four types in high strength. Here the figures are less than ten and two percent respectively. In simple language, extensive mixing of regional types at high parity levels is very uncommon. Moderate level counties demonstrate these same patterns, but with less emphasis.

TABLE 12

Specific Matchings of High and Moderate Strength Counties among the Four Major Types of Religious Groupings

NUMBER OF COUNTIES WITH PAIRED ASSOCIATIONS BETWEEN TWO TYPES					
	HIGH STRENGTH Type			MODERATE STRENGTH Type		
	2	3	4	2	3	4
Type 1	2	10	10	26	85	35
Type 2	—	13	18	—	77	34
Type 3	—	—	7	—	—	112

NUMBER OF COUNTIES WITH ASSOCIATIONS AMONG THREE TYPES					
	HIGH STRENGTH Types			MODERATE STRENGTH Types		
	2+3	3+4	2+4	2+3	3+4	2+4
Type 1	4	4	2	15	10	15
Type 2	—	4	—	—	11	—

NOTE: High and moderate strength for a type of religious grouping in a county are defined operationally as less than and more than one standard deviation above the mean factor score per county for each type respectively.

Table 12 allows inspection of the specific matchings of shared counties between the four types of religious groupings. Here again high and moderate counties are treated separately. This time the table reveals the number of county units in which either particular pairs or sets of three religious groupings appear. Obviously Type 3, the native American Calvinist Churches that predominate in western states, are the most geographically diverse set. This denominational grouping is twice as likely as any other type to share moderate strength turf with another major national type of religious grouping. Its strongest association is with Type 4, the northeastern and metropolitan type. Conversely, this table, like the one before it, shows a high degree of disassociation between Types 1 and 2. These share only two high category counties in common and only 36 moderate category counties, comprising less than one percent of all the counties in the nation. Turning to the high and moderate associations among three types (the lower portion of the table), the most important aspect of the table is the small number of cases. There are a mere 18 counties in the entire continental United States in which any three of these types of religious groupings share high strength. Similarly, there are only 51 counties in which any three of these types of groupings share moderate levels of strength.

The foregoing set of maps and tables have allowed a more detailed view of the nature of religious regionalism in the United States than has previously been possible. Let us briefly summarize the central findings of this examination. First, simply by virtue of the sheer number of counties in which each type of religious grouping is located, it is impossible to claim that the turfs they occupy are mutually exclusive. There are, beyond question, many counties in which multiple types are found. However, in spite of this fact, there are some important elements of geographical separateness between the four major types of religious groupings. Most of the counties in which all four sets of denominations exhibit high or moderate strength are *not* similarly occupied by another of the four types. Roughly two percent of all the counties in the nation contain high levels of adherents for more than one set of denominations. Thus, while on the one hand very few counties contain only one denominational type, relatively few counties contain two or more with high degrees of strength and numerical parity. As will be seen in the next chapter, these dual characteristics of American religious regionalism have some important consequences for the parameters of America's religious pluralism. However, before leaving the subject of religious regionalism it seems imperative that we compare the regional, theological, and ethnic characteristics of the typology developed here to those of previous researchers.

THE REGIONAL TYPOLOGIES COMPARED

The denominational groupings introduced in Chapter 3 have now been portrayed in detail both cartographically and in terms of their historical, social, and theological consistencies. Clearly the picture that has emerged is both similar to and different from those regionalizations presented earlier by Zelinsky and Shortridge. While a methodological comparison is offered in Chapter 3, a substantive comparison of the three regionalizations concerns us here. The three sets of regions or types are presented in a summary manner in Table 13. At first glance, the labels themselves do not provide much guidance because each typology identifies groupings or regions according to different criteria. When examined more closely, however, the degree of similarity or difference between the different systems becomes readily identifiable.

For example, Zelinsky, starting from the premise that certain of the conventionally identified regions of the country have a distinctive denominational composition, identifies a region labelled "South." Shortridge, starting from a

TABLE 13

Congruence of Religious Regionalizations as Proposed by Zelinsky, Shortridge, and Newman & Halvorson

ZELINSKY	SHORTRIDGE	NEWMAN & HALVORSON
PRIMARY REGIONS	PRIMARY REGIONS	PRIMARY REGIONS
New England & Mid Atlantic	Catholic	Northeast & Metropolitan "Triple-Melting Pot"
Upper Midwest	Diverse Liberal Protestant	Midwest & Northwest Northern European Protestant
Southern	Intense Conservative Protestant	Southern Anglo-Calvinist
Western	Diverse Liberal Protestant	Central & Western "Native" Anglo-Protestant
SECONDARY REGIONS	SECONDARY REGIONS	SECONDARY REGIONS
Mormon	Intense Conservative Protestant	
Spanish Catholic	Super-Catholic	
	Intense Conservative Protestant	German Pietists Dutch Reformed

NOTE: Shortridge uses a "transitional" category, which by definition does not conform to the kinds of categories in the other two typologies. However, the counties in his "transitional" type would very likely appear as residual counties if our factor grouping maps had been drawn to designate counties neither high nor moderately high for any given denominational grouping.

procedure which, among other things, sorts liberal and conservative Protestant groups, identifies a configuration of conservative Protestantism in the deep South that is quite similar. Our own typology specifies a grouping of southern Anglo-Calvinists that occupy a similar space, and are virtually the same set of denominations as those specified by Shortridge. Clearly, despite the differences in procedure and labels, each of the three typologies identifies this same feature and region in this case.

Zelinsky identifies a midwestern region, yet he also states that "the Middle West fails completely to assert itself in terms of a distinctive constellation of religions . . ." (Zelinsky, 1973: 99). His failure to find such distinctiveness stems from his technique of mapping families of denominations that share a common label and is clearly contradicted by both Shortridge and by the regionalization presented here. Shortridge identifies a midwestern grouping of "diverse liberal Protestants" and states that it is quite similar to that of Zelinsky (Shortridge 1977). In contrast, two of the groupings identified in our typology occupy different parts of the Midwest. The continental Reformation grouping, which is primarily located in the upper portion of the Midwest, helps to identify not only a geographic or regional entity but a "distinctive constellation of religions" and is consistent with Shortridge. The western, native, Protestant denominational grouping occupies a significant portion of the lower Midwest and central Plains regions. This grouping coincides with Shortridge's typology and provides another identity for Zelinsky's "elusive" distinctiveness. Similarly, Zelinsky identifies a western region, but asserts that it also lacks a "distinctive constellation of religions" (Zelinsky, 1973: 99). Shortridge ignores Zelinsky's statement and stresses the similarity between Zelinsky's configuration and the western segment of his liberal diverse Protestant group. While several major groupings in our own typology have West Coast representation, the third type, or native Calvinist grouping is the most clearly western in orientation.

The lack of agreement among the three typologies concerning the existence and degree of distinctiveness of the midwestern and western regions raises an important general issue. Simply stated, Zelinsky claims separate western and midwestern regions but has difficulty giving them distinct religious identities. Shortridge, ignores these alleged regional-cultural boundaries and assigns one large "diverse liberal Protestant" grouping to Zelinsky's two areas. Our typology identifies two distinct ethno-religious groupings that divide this geographic space still differently. Our midwestern group actually stretches from the upper Midwest thru the Northwest. Our western group extends from the southern tier of the Midwest, through the central plains states to California.

The implications of these differences may be summarized as follows. If Zelinsky's approach is accurate, the other two typologies fail to identify correctly the religious content of these traditional, widely recognized regions. However, if the two types of religious groupings really are culturally salient, and are more widespread, covering several of the traditional regions of the country, these traditional culture regions so often used by cultural geographers and other social scientists may be inappropriate for the analysis of religion and thus be obsolete.

Carrying this line of argument further, Zelinsky identifies separate regions labelled "New England" and "Middle Atlantic" which do not really emerge from the procedures employed either by Shortridge or by us. The Catholic-Protestant dichotomy utilized by Shortridge isolates an area identified as Catholic in the Northeast. Unfortunately, that designation obscures relationships to a number of other significant denominational groups possessing very similar patterns. The northeastern grouping identified by our analysis includes not only Catholics, but also Episcopalian and Jewish groups, as well as others associated with metropolitan areas. Furthermore, this grouping extends over both the northeastern and New England regions identified by Zelinsky as separate entities.

Finally, each of the regionalizations identifies a series of "islands" or relatively small clusters of locally dominant denominations. Not surprisingly there are both similarities and differences. Zelinsky's identification of the Catholic area in southern Louisiana coincides with the "Super Catholic" designation of that region by Shortridge. The Mormon area identified by Zelinsky appears as an enclave in Shortridge's "intense conservative Protestant" cluster. Our typology identifies two secondary groupings. The German Pietist type coincides with Zelinsky's Pennsylvania German. The Dutch Reformed grouping is not identified by either Shortridge or Zelinsky. It bears reemphasis that both of these types are interpreted as non-national. Both statistically and substantively they are less important than the four primary national configurations. Zelinsky notes islands in the Carolinas and in Texas, both of which appear as outliers on the relevant factor maps presented here. However, these do not show up in Shortridge's typology. Thus the pattern with regard to the so-called "islands" is rather inconsistent. Yet the fact that some of them emerge from each of the approaches to regionalization indicates the general reality of such features in certain localities.

Two additional elements of the new typology proposed here remain to be stressed. First, it must be reiterated that although each of the four national types of groupings identified and mapped here possess certain discrete areas of primary strength, they also are present in virtually all the counties of the country. Consequently, at least some of the distinctiveness of these regions is more apparent than real. Furthermore, for all of these types, a small but still significant degree of overlapping occurs with the areas of strength of the various other types. This is particularly pronounced in the case of the third group, the western, native Protestants that occupy the space between the first two types and the fourth, i.e., the northeastern type. These two factors further point to the necessarily arbitrary quality of all regionalization schemes. They are sometimes misleading in situations with as much diversity and freedom of both movement and affiliation as are encountered in the United States.

What then, by way of summary, may be suggested on the basis of the foregoing analysis? First, when allowed to locate themselves throughout the space of the nation's counties, denominations emerge in configurations that do not necessarily conform to either a "families" approach or to certain presumed theological differences. Furthermore, it becomes apparent that Catholics do not stand alone and isolated, but in fact share a distributional pattern with a number of major Protestant groups and with Jews. The groupings thus generated do, moreover, make a great deal of sense when viewed from an historical viewpoint, emphasizing their origins and the migration history of the country. Furthermore, the groups express a decipherable national regionalization similar in some ways to those advanced by Zelinsky and Shortridge, although it springs from a different point of origin. This pattern of regions is a bit less distinct than certain patterns used in the past. However, it adds both a new dimension to an understanding of the regional flavor of the various religious configurations and suggests some reason for qualifying previous claims for the discrete regionalization of American religion.

5

The Complexities of Pluralism

RELIGION AS A MEASURE OF CULTURE

This chapter presents a detailed examination of patterns of religious pluralism in the United States as well as changes in those patterns for the 1952-1971 period. An interest in the phenomena of pluralism was an important motivating factor in our original desire to work with these data. In the course of our work we would learn as much about the problems of measuring pluralism as about pluralism itself. This is not to suggest that the present chapter has little to say about American religious pluralism. On the contrary, as we initially anticipated, these census-type data for American religious groups unquestionably afford a view of patterns in pluralism that have not previously been depicted with survey research data. However, just as we had not predicted the degree of stability in these data from 1952 to 1971, so the emerging patterns of pluralism, regardless of how measured, are different from what we anticipated. As with some of the other major, aggregate trends already depicted, geographic patterns of religious pluralism do not exactly conform to the conventional wisdom about how these patterns "ought" to look. However, before presenting these patterns, we must first consider the methodological problems and choices involved in shaping them.

It has become a commonplace view in the sciences that one's methods frequently determine one's findings. For instance, as we discussed in Chapter 3, Shortridge's separation of the data for Catholics from that of the Protestant groups predetermined the existence of certain "Catholic" regional entities. Similarly, the kinds of methodological choices we made pointed us in the direction of some different findings on the question of religious regions than those offered by Shortridge. In this chapter we shall present

and compare several different cartographic displays of pluralism patterns. Each of them is based upon slightly different assumptions about what these data actually mean and how they should be manipulated and interpreted. However, each of these several methodological choices is based on one fundamental assumption that social scientists routinely make about the cultural significance of religious affiliation. We turn now to an examination of that assumption.

The assumption that must be examined here is, in fact, articulated by Zelinsky (1961) in the very first sentence of his essay on the 1952 NCCC data. He says, "Almost all human geographers will accept the truism that among the phenomena forming or reflecting the areal differences in cultures with which they are so intimately concerned, few are as potent and sensitive as religion" (1961:139). Of course, we need not trace this assertion to Zelinsky's door. He is correct in saying that most social geographers and, indeed, most social scientists assume that religion either shapes or reflects secular culture and subcultures in powerful ways. We have already seen in Chapter 3 that an equally common assumption about the degree of discrete regionalism among denominations was not quite true. In part, the factor analysis technique solved this problem by indicating a way of viewing denominations in culturally distinct groupings. However, it now is necessary to ask again to what degree either denominations or groups of them can be viewed as culturally meaningful, or as measures of different cultural entities?

Let us first deal with the issue of denominational level measures. These census-type data, as well as all survey and sample data that rely upon denominational labels as measures of religion, all contain certain flaws. First, among both Catholics and Jews there are important ethnic, and therefore, cultural differences, that are concealed within the single denominational label. Among American Jews, researchers have long stressed the cultural and even social class differences between German Jews and more recent eastern European immigrant groups. These ethnic differences are routinely expressed in denominational differences within Judaism, the eastern Europeans tending toward Orthodox practice, and the more secularized Germanic Jews following the Reform tradition. Of course, with Jews constituting only about three percent of the general population there have been relatively few studies of the secular and cultural consequences of these differences. As far as the issue of cultural pluralism is involved, a much more serious measurement problem arises in the case of Roman Catholics.

Catholics account for nearly one-third of the religious adherents in the 1952 data file, and almost 50 percent of those in the 1971 study. However, it is sheer nonsense to treat Catholicism as a monolithic religious or cultural entity. Important cultural differences exist not only between so-called racial groupings within the Church (Cuban, Puerto Rican, and Mexican) but equally among the European groups as well. As Abramson (1973) has shown, German, Irish, French, and Italian Catholics not only cling to different ethnic cultures, but they all practice Catholicism differently from one another. Regrettably, there is no way of measuring the ethnic diversity within denominational level Catholic data. Most researchers, ourselves included, have simply assumed that certain pronounced areas on the Catholic distribution maps conform to historic differences in ethnic immigration. In other words, it seems safe enough to assume that much of the Catholicism in Louisiana and Maine is ethnically French; in the Southwest and West, Mexican; and in Florida, Cuban or Puerto Rican. However, in those places where one assumes European Catholics are most numerous and most culturally diverse, the Northeast and New England, the data do not measure that diversity. To make matters more complicated, these same areas probably exhibit significant racial diversity, and thus additional cultural diversity, among the Catholic population. While we state these assumptions and conceptually take note of them, as long as one works with denominational data it is not possible to repair these shortcomings in precise statistical ways.

Obviously, we are not the first researchers to note these difficulties. One suspects that these problems were an element in Shortridge's decision to separate Catholic from Protestant statistics in searching for religious regions. By isolating the distribution for Catholics he could at least make explicit his assumptions, as Zelinski also does, about the ethnic divisions in that data in some parts of the nation. However, as has been shown in our own typology, Shortridge's choice prevented him from identifying important statistical relationships between the distribution of Catholics and those of certain other major denominations. In any event, as maps of religious pluralism

are examined in this chapter, one must be mindful of the degree to which ethnic and cultural differences among Catholics simply cannot be measured by denominational level data. This limitation applies regardless of whether these patterns of pluralism are based upon denominational level data or upon higher level aggregations such as the typology developed in Chapters 3 and 4.

Unfortunately, there is an equally serious problem of measurement contained in the data for Protestant denominations. If the Catholic data underestimate cultural differences, the Protestant denominational labels tend to overestimate them. Stated differently, in some cases a variety of denominational differences among the Protestants reflect minor historical and theological disputes between groups embodying the same general cultural values and traditions. In other words, while Greeley (1972a), Newman (1973), and many other students of America's pluralism justifiably claim that religious denominations are ethnic entities, these ethno-religious entities are not all completely different and distinct from one another.

Classic illustrations of this point are contained in at least two of the factor groupings identified in Chapter 3. The Christian Reformed Church and the Reformed Church in America, the two denominations in Type 6, are derived from a single previous denomination. Culturally, both denominations represent the Dutch branch of Presbyterianism in the United States. While these two denominations are culturally the same, they would be counted as different entities in any scrutiny of pluralism patterns in which cultural entities are equated with individual denominational names. Another example of this relates to the fifth grouping in our typology, which essentially represents the several branches of German Pietism in the United States. Indeed, the Mennonites, the two Brethren denominations, the Evangelical Congregational Church, and even the ethnically Swedish Evangelical Covenant Church are all followers of the German Pietist tradition. These groups all emerged from what were significant theological disputes at the time of their respective formations. However, in the contemporary American context it is difficult to argue that they exhibit significant religio-cultural differentiation. This particular assortment of denominations is associated statistically precisely because of their cultural uniformity.

It is clear then, that denominational level data, whether for Catholics, Protestants, or Jews, contain some major slippages as measures of culture differences. While denominations are cultural entities, they cannot simply be equated with cultural differences on a one for one basis. To do so sometimes alleges more cultural differences than really exist, and at other times hides those that are most socially salient. Nonetheless, with this warning in mind, we will now present and discuss several alternative depictions of pluralism patterns based on different techniques of analysis using these data.

SOME ALTERNATE PATTERNS IN PLURALISM

The foregoing discussion of problems in measuring pluralism with these denominational data might easily breed some skepticism about attempting such analyses. However, there are far more important and useful implications of these issues. Recognizing that all denominational data and composite measures based upon such data have certain limitations, it seems prudent to approach the question of pluralism in several different ways. Rather than opting for one set of measures of pluralism, we can balance several different pictures of reality through the countervailing influences of the advantages and shortcomings of each view. That is the strategy of analysis in this chapter. Three different cartographic depictions of America's religious and cultural pluralism are examined and compared.

The first and simplest approach is to grant each denomination equal status as a religio-cultural variable. In this approach the numbers of adherents per denomination per county do *not* enter into the calculations. Rather, we are simply concerned with how many different denominations appear from one county to the next. Obviously, counties with high numbers of denominations in them are defined as highly pluralistic. Those in which few individual denominations are represented are understood as less pluralistic. This particular approach of course, risks overestimating the cultural diversity inherent in the many Protestant denominations. Yet, as will be seen on Maps 8 and 9, the images produced by this use of these data conform to certain other features of these data already discussed.

Maps 8 and 9 have been constructed in the same manner as all the previous maps presented both here and in the earlier *Atlas*. In this instance the raw data consist of the number of denominations represented in each of the 3073 counties. These data have then been trichotomized into high, middle, and low thirds, represented by the three shaded areas on the maps. Map 8 provides this information for 1971, and Map 9 provides the percentage change between 1952 and 1971 for the same data. These two maps provide a first depiction of pluralism in 1971 and changes in pluralism between 1952 and 1971.

When calculated in this way, the map for degrees of pluralism in 1971 appears to be a relatively close analogue to a basic United States population map. Accordingly, it is also quite similar to Map 1, the 1971 base map for total religious adherence presented in Chapter 2. In fact, the similarities of these maps suggest that in the aggregate religious adherence is closely tied to population density. Simply stated the more people in a county, the more people claiming religious adherence in that county, and the more different brands of religion in that county. As will be seen in Chapter 6, a regression analysis of the relationship between these religious data and United States Census data provides verification of such propositions. However, for the moment, even if one grants the underestimation of cultural differences among Catholics, and the overestimation of cultural differentiation among the Protestants, Maps 8 and 9 still make a great deal of sense.

Turning first to Map 8, counties falling in the highest category in 1971 are most prevalent in the Northeast. Elsewhere these counties are typically located in metropolitan areas. Thus, even with the measurement difficulties noted, this depiction of pluralism patterns is consistent with what one would have expected to encounter. It is equally important to note that the lower numerical limit for this first category is only eleven denominations per county. In other words, the most pluralistic counties in the nation include a relatively low number of denominations. This finding is consistent with the analysis of regionalism provided in Chapter 4. There it was shown that relatively few of the high and moderate strength counties for any of the four major types of denominational groupings are shared by another of the groupings. In this sense the data in Map 8, depicting the number of individual denominations (not groupings) per county, reflect these previous findings.

Counties in the lowest third (containing fewer than seven denominations each) are largely found in the Southeast, and in the Great Plains and Rocky Mountains. This pattern also meshes with certain previous findings. It is widely recognized that the United States Census reports show these three areas to be less populous and less urbanized. However, this category on the map also reflects the geographic features of Type 2, the southern grouping of denominations. Again, in Chapter 4 it was seen that this denominational grouping, containing only four denominations in 1971, has the least high category geographic overlap with other denominational groupings. In that regard we also noted in Chapter 3 that factor loadings for Type 2 suggest increasing religio-cultural homogeneity for the 1952-1971 period. With so many low category counties in the regional space of Type 2, this first depiction of pluralism patterns does in fact, confirm that earlier impression.

Given the stability of most of the religious patterns examined for the 1952-1971 period, we have again chosen not to map the 1952 data here. However, Table 14 provides a concise statistical summary of the trichotomized sets of data for pluralism in 1952 and 1971. Specifically, it compares the category limits (numbers of denominations per county) and the number of counties in these categories for both sets of data. With the exception of a change of one digit in the middle category limit (from 7-10 to 7-11), these are virtually unchanged for the 1952-1971 period. This degree of stability is quite remarkable. Between 1950 and 1970 half of the counties in the United States declined in population. Moreover, those that did not decline registered an aggregate growth rate of 35 percent (see Table 2). In this context the data in Table 14 reflect impressive locational stability in terms of numbers of religious denominations per county.

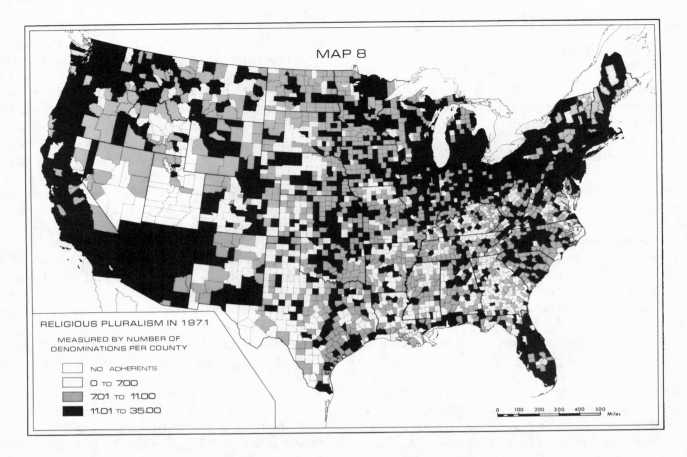

MAP 8

RELIGIOUS PLURALISM IN 1971

MEASURED BY NUMBER OF
DENOMINATIONS PER COUNTY

NO ADHERENTS

0 TO 7.00

7.01 TO 11.00

11.01 TO 35.00

0 100 200 300 400 500
Miles

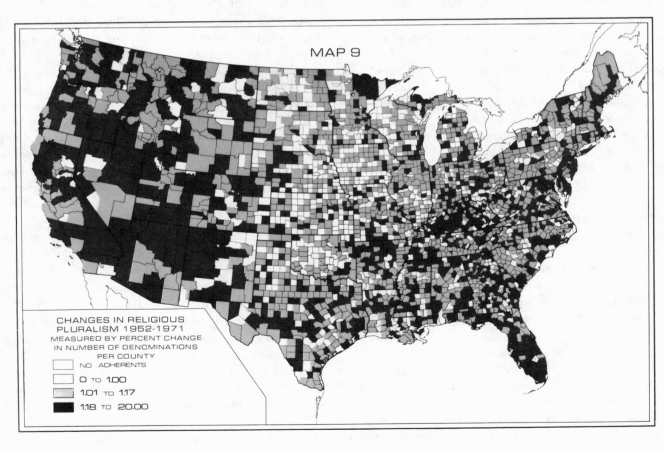

MAP 9

CHANGES IN RELIGIOUS
PLURALISM 1952-1971
MEASURED BY PERCENT CHANGE
IN NUMBER OF DENOMINATIONS
PER COUNTY
NO ADHERENTS

0 TO 1.00

1.01 TO 1.17

1.18 TO 20.00

The data for percentage change in pluralism contained in Map 9 reinforce the impression of stability given by Table 14. The lowest category on this map appears in 627 of the 3073 counties in the nation. That category represents counties that either decreased in pluralism (i.e., lost denominations) or remained stable (i.e., no change in number of denominations). Thus, during a period when half of the counties in the United States declined in population, only one-fifth of all counties decreased in religious pluralism as measured here. However, as would be expected, these counties of declining pluralism are located in places known to be marked by the out-migration of rural populations, especially on the Great Plains and in the deep South. The middle category on Map 9 represents moderate increases in pluralism. There are several significant features of these counties. First, there is a disproportionately large number of them, 1400. That is slightly less than half the counties in the nation indicating very minor shifts in the degree of pluralism for a nearly twenty year period. Moreover, because of the limited range of the data itself (0-35) a change in only a few denominations per county registers as a significant percentage change. In other words, this measure of change tends to exaggerate what are really minor shifts. Thus the real image conveyed by Map 9 is stability. Finally, this is a very non-regionalized pattern of stability; counties registering such changes are widely dispersed across the nation.

TABLE 14
Number of Denominations per County in 1952 and 1971 according to Trichotomous Category Limits, and Numbers of Counties per Category

	Lower Third	Middle Third	Upper Third
1952			
Denominations per County	0-7	7-10	10-35
No. of Counties	945	868	1262
1971			
Denominations per County	0-7	7-11	11-35
No. of Counties	781	1127	1167

The high category counties may next be examined. Here a more discernable regional pattern emerges. Counties in which significant increases in the degree of pluralism have occurred are common in the Southeast and even more so in the western states. The southeastern clusters appear in the Virginia-Carolina Piedmont, and stretch into Florida and Texas. In the western states strong increases are found in Colorado and New Mexico, as well as throughout southern and central California. Smaller areas of high increases in pluralism also register in Utah, Nevada, Idaho and northern Arizona. Such counties are far less common in the Northeast, and when found, seem to be confined to non-metropolitan locations.

In summary, a first measure of religious pluralism and changes in pluralism between 1952 and 1971, based upon the number of denominations per county and percentage changes in that measure, provides a general pattern of stability. In 1971, pluralism, like the density of religious adherence, is most pronounced in the denser population corridors, especially in the Northeast. Conversely, increases in pluralism are most common in those parts of the nation where population has grown over the 1950-1970 period. However, the change patterns here are a less exact reflection of population trends than the 1971 data for religious pluralism. This first measure of religious pluralism and changes in pluralism both confirms and belies our expectations. We anticipated that religio-cultural pluralism would be a function of population density and growth. That expectation is confirmed. However, based on the general perception that the 1950-1970 period produced major kinds of population shifts in American society, we anticipated similarly dramatic shifts in patterns of religious pluralism. While changes in pluralism did follow population growth, on the whole such changes were not very dramatic. Indeed, this first measure of pluralism suggests not much change for the nearly twenty year period.

A second approach to the measurement of pluralism and changes in pluralism involves calculating both the number of denominations per county and the relative sizes of the adherence in those denominations at the county level. There are several kinds of statistical measures available that will achieve this kind of computation with these data. For instance, Shortridge (1977) has used an index of concentration for this purpose. This is essentially the same measure as we described in Chapter 2, and used there to examine elements of geographic stability in the two data sets. In the present case we have used a similar measure, called an entropy index (Shannon and Weaver 1949). Like the index of concentration, the entropy measure is basically derived from the Lorenz curve, and calibrates the degree to which a real distribution departs from an hypothesized norm within which the distribution is even. In this case, this assumption would mean that the total membership within a county would be evenly divided among the various denominations. Clearly such a case of parity would indicate a certain type of pluralism. County units within which a single denomination or a small set of denominations dominates the distribution could not be described as genuinely pluralistic.

The index values for the entropy measure range from 0 to 1. Low values represent very uneven distributions, or low levels of pluralism. Conversely, high values indicate more even distributions between denominational adherents and thus higher levels of pluralism. As before, the raw data (this time scores calculated by the entropy index) have been trichotomized, and maps for both the 1971 and 1952-1971 change distributions have been created. Also, we have again retained the statistical data for the 1952 and 1971 distributions in tabular form (Table 15). Let us next ex-

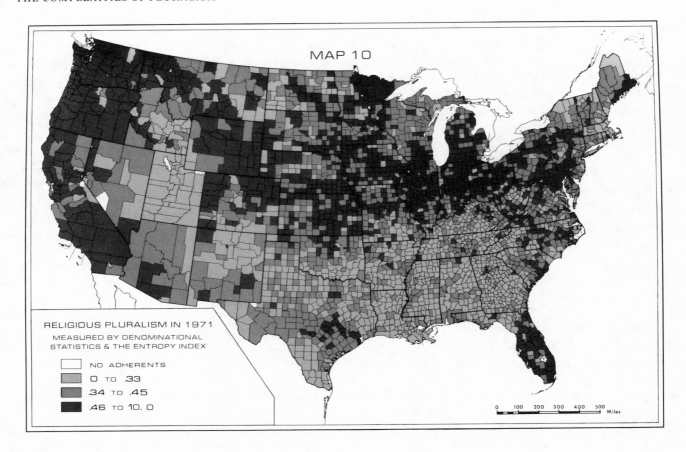

MAP 10

RELIGIOUS PLURALISM IN 1971

MEASURED BY DENOMINATIONAL
STATISTICS & THE ENTROPY INDEX

NO ADHERENTS

0 TO .33

.34 TO .45

.46 TO 10. 0

0   100   200   300   400   500
                                 Miles

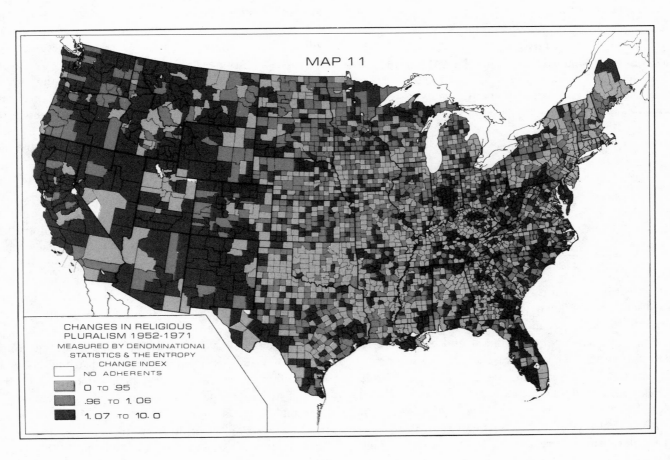

MAP 11

CHANGES IN RELIGIOUS
PLURALISM 1952-1971

MEASURED BY DENOMINATIONAL
STATISTICS & THE ENTROPY
CHANGE INDEX

NO ADHERENTS

0 TO .95

.96 TO 1. 06

1. 07 TO 10. 0

amine pluralism patterns derived from this more complex use of denominational measures.

The patterns of pluralism and changes in pluralism revealed by the denominational level entropy measure are displayed in Maps 10 and 11. Map 10, depicting pluralism in 1971, is somewhat different from what might have been expected either from conventional wisdom or from the preceding maps just discussed. When measured in this fashion, pluralism does not appear to be high in the northeastern urban areas—where it actually appears to be low. This apparent anomaly can be attributed in part, to the denominational base of measurement. As noted earlier, the label "Catholic" masks pluralism because it covers such a wide range of ethnic types. Since Catholics comprise half of all adherents in 1971, and are very strongly represented in the Northeast, they tend to deflate the entropy measure, creating an apparent lack of pluralism in that area. Obviously, it is far more congruent with popular stereotypes to find areas of low pluralism stretching across the Southeast in a relatively solid pattern, as they do on Map 10. These counties extend from Georgia to Texas and Oklahoma, while additional areas of low pluralism are found in New Mexico and Utah as well.

As might be expected, the areas of highest pluralism for 1971 on this map reflect the problem of overcounting the degree of cultural diversity represented by the many Protestant denominations. We have previously noted that only a small number of religious denominations are present in large numbers of counties. This means that many zero cases are calculated in the entropy index. The result is a rather low set of values for the entire range of the entropy scores being mapped. Nonetheless, areas of high pluralism emerge in rather predictable places, especially considering the disproportionate influence of Protestant denominations upon the index. High category counties are prevalent in the Midwest, stretching from Ohio to Wisconsin and Iowa, and into the Pacific Northwest. Stated differently, this way of measuring pluralism emphasizes the mixing of large Continental Protestant denominations, precisely those characteristic of Type 1. It is not without importance that Type 1 accounts for roughly half of the explained variance in both time periods (see Table 8). In simple terms, for the several reasons just stated, we are inclined to interpret Map 10 as more of a representation of Protestant denominational pluralism than of either general religious or cultural pluralism. However, given the traditional focus in American society upon Anglo-Protestant culture, these data serve a useful purpose in pointing to the vitality and significance of immigrant continental Churches in the structure of contemporary American society.

The remaining high pluralism counties on Map 10 offer a mixed pattern. Certain areas one might have predicted as being high by any measure of pluralism are in fact so. Included among these are southern Florida, central Arizona, and both southern and central California. However, these are easily offset by high pluralism counties in numerous locations that are genuinely anomalous to this particular set of measurement strategies.

The patterns of change in pluralism as measured by the entropy index with denominational level data conform a bit more closely to both our expectations and to patterns portrayed by Map 9. The low category on Map 11, indicating a decrease in the level of pluralism, is strongly represented in the Northeast, particularly in the urbanized corridor. There is also a scattering of such counties dispersed throughout the Southeast and the Great Plains, particularly in Texas and Oklahoma. This pattern is consistent with patterns of population decline in those regions.

The pattern of increase is not very sharply defined, although a few readily identifiable areas emerge, among them the middle Atlantic states, the Carolina Piedmont, south Florida, and central Indiana. To the degree that any region emerges from this rather mixed pattern it is the West, particularly California and the entire Pacific Northwest. However, the intermixture of categories within regions militates against neat regionalization. Why is this so?

This rather jumbled pattern of change is explained to some degree by the fact that relatively little change in pluralism levels has apparently taken place over the nearly twenty year interval. This stability has been discussed in numerous contexts in earlier chapters. As shown in Table 15, there was virtually no change in the category limits, means, or standard deviations of the trichotomized 1952 and 1971 denominational based entropy distributions. This pattern of stability is consistent with many of our earlier findings relative to denominational patterns. It is clear that relatively minor shifts begin to assume somewhat larger proportions when viewed on the maps. This characteristic is compounded by the fact that smaller and less pluralistic areas in 1952 are likely to be far more sensitive to changes when measured in this fashion. Viewed in this light, the somewhat scattered pluralism change pattern on Map 11 is quite understandable.

TABLE 15

Entropy Levels for Trichotomized 1952 and 1971 Denominational Data

	LOWER THIRD	MIDDLE THIRD	UPPER THIRD	$\overline{X}$	S.D.
1952	0 - .32	.32 - .44	.44 & above	.38	.13
1971	0 - .33	.33 - .45	.45 & above	.38	.13

Thus far, two different cartographic depictions of patterns of pluralism in 1971 and changes in pluralism patterns for 1952-1971 have been examined. The first of these confirms expectations, in that the Northeast appears most pluralistic. Generally speaking, patterns of religio-cultural pluralism and changes in them seem to follow patterns of general population density and change. However, the

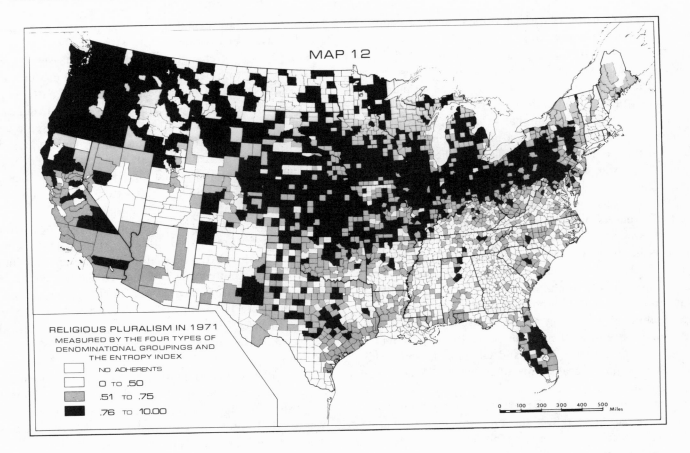

MAP 12

RELIGIOUS PLURALISM IN 1971
MEASURED BY THE FOUR TYPES OF
DENOMINATIONAL GROUPINGS AND
THE ENTROPY INDEX

☐   NO ADHERENTS
☐   0 TO .50
▨   .51 TO .75
■   .76 TO 10.00

0 100 200 300 400 500
Miles

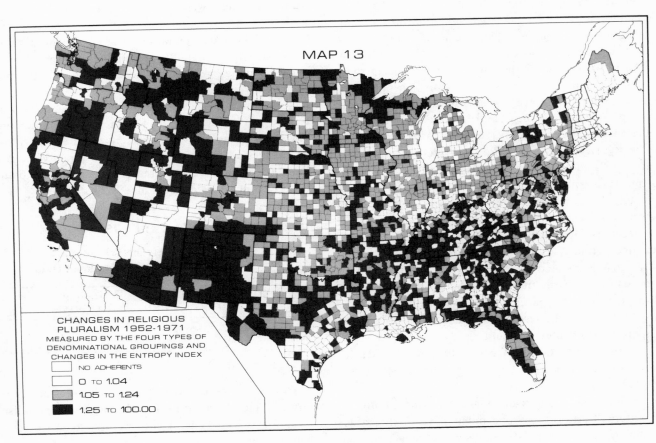

MAP 13

CHANGES IN RELIGIOUS
PLURALISM 1952-1971
MEASURED BY THE FOUR TYPES OF
DENOMINATIONAL GROUPINGS AND
CHANGES IN THE ENTROPY INDEX

☐   NO ADHERENTS
☐   0 TO 1.04
▨   1.05 TO 1.24
■   1.25 TO 100.00

measure employed here, the number of denominations per county, is regrettably simplistic. A second set of measurement techniques proved a bit less satisfying. Here an entropy index was used to calculate a statistic that involved both the number of denominations per county and the relative sizes of those denominations at the county level (see Table 15). However, it is clear that this strategy of measurement tends to maximize the several kinds of distortions of cultural differences inherent in religious denominational data. To a large extent, for reasons already discussed, this second set of maps is probably a better depiction of Protestant pluralism than religio-cultural pluralism. The final set of maps, that are presented next, provide a partial resolution of these measurement problems.

Throughout Chapters 3 and 4 it has been argued that the types of denominational groupings generated by the factor analysis technique are meaningful religio-cultural entities. They exhibit distinct theological, ethnic, and regional patterns. In all these regards they represent socially meaningful and statistically valid ways of transforming the diverse assortment of denominational statistics into more general religio-cultural entities. Four of the six groupings have been shown to be of major significance for national patterns of religious regionalism. Three of these four exhibit remarkable internal homogeneity when viewed as cultural (ethno-religious) entities. The fourth of these, while internally diverse, can be described as representing a particular, somewhat secularistic ethos (i.e., the triple melting pot). In short, these four culturally identifiable types provide a highly appropriate set of variables to use in studying patterns of religio-cultural pluralism. Using these four types as cultural variables may reduce the several problems of distortion inherent in the denominational level data. The next set of maps show the results of entering these four types into the entropy and entropy change indexing procedures already described in this chapter.

The pluralism patterns and pluralism change patterns produced by entering the four denominational groupings into the entropy and entropy change procedures are depicted on Maps 12 and 13. The 1971 pattern is sharply defined. With the number of cases per county reduced from the 35 denominations to only four types of groupings, the values of the entropy index have risen sharply over those on Map 10. This results from the relative absence of zero cases in the overwhelming majority of counties across the country. However, the pattern of pluralism portrayed here is only slightly different from that produced in Map 10 by the denominational level data. The low areas again appear primarily in the Southeast, stretching from the Carolinas and Virginia across the old South into east Texas. Secondary pockets of low levels of pluralism again appear in New England, New Mexico, and Utah, as well as in south Texas. The high values are sharply differentiated and appear primarily in a band across the Midwest. They extend from western Pennsylvania and Ohio through

Indiana, Illinois, and Michigan, and finally into Wisconsin. That pattern begins to be interrupted, but still extends into the central and northern Great Plains, reappearing rather strongly in Washington and Oregon. The northern bias of this pattern is most clear in the distinction between the northern and southern Plains areas, and between the Pacific Northwest and California. Thus, although the pattern is somewhat clearer than that on the denomination-based map, it is a very similar distribution and continues to reflect patterns of Protestant pluralism more than general religio-cultural pluralism.

Just as the entropy pattern for 1971 based on the four types is more sharply defined than its denomination-based counterpart, the new entropy change map (Map 13) makes a bit more sense in regional terms than its predecessor (Map 11). Counties of the lowest category, some of which show a modest increase in pluralism, are largely found in two sorts of areas. First, they appear in those areas that were already pluralistic by the early 1950s. Included are the northeastern urban corridor, particularly New York and New Jersey, and parts of the Midwest, including Ohio, Indiana, Illinois, and Michigan. These low category counties are also scattered through those areas experiencing stable or declining populations during the 1950-1970 period, notably in the Southeast and the Great Plains. Counties in the high category are distributed in a fashion much like those on Map 11. They appear in the middle Atlantic states and are scattered across the Southeast, interspersed between counties in the lowest category. Evidently this reflects differences between rural and urban segments of that region. Areas of the Gulf Coast and Texas that experienced rapid increase in general population also show up, as do similar areas in New Mexico, southern Arizona, and the Pacific Northwest. Surprisingly, although some areas of California carry this designation, they generally fall outside of the largest metropolitan areas.

TABLE 16

Entropy Levels for Trichotomized 1952 and 1971 Data Based on Four National Groupings

	LOWER THIRD	MIDDLE THIRD	UPPER THIRD	X̄	S.D.
1952	0 - .43	.43 - .68	.68 & above	.54	.28
1971	0 - .50	.50 - .75	.75 & above	.60	.27

It should be noted that the range of change in pluralism reported by this calculation is rather different from either of the previous portrayals of change in the level of pluralism. When viewed from the perspective of these four national associations of denominations, the overall picture is one of pervasive increases in the level of pluralism, with the high changes standing out as quite appreciable. Statistical evidence of this trend is provided in Table 16. The table provides the value ranges, means, and standard deviations for the trichotomized data based on the entropy scores for the four denominational groupings. This table in part reflects the more "compact" nature of this measure when calculated with only four instead of 35 variables. However, it may also again indicate a sort of enhanced reality derived from viewing the data in this fashion. Conventional wisdom concerning demographic and cultural change in the country leads one to expect changes of the sort that only this measure provides.

In summary, it must be reiterated that none of the patterns of religious pluralism portrayed here are quite what one would expect in terms of general cultural pluralism in the country. Clearly the excessive denominationalism among Protestant groups serves to over-emphasize pluralistic tendencies in areas dominated by such groups. Conversely, Catholicism tends to mask much of the real diversity in areas within which Catholics are a major group. Any attempt to use denominational measures of religion as cultural variables, as has been done here, is bound to encounter certain limitations and in some ways contradict more broadly held notions about diversity within the cultural regions of the nation. While this may diminish the utility of such portrayals, it also illustrates the degree to which religious diversity and cultural diversity demand careful and to a degree separate analyses.

6
The Social Causes of Denominational Patterns

SELECTING SOCIAL INDICATORS

The interactions between religious groups and the societies in which they are found is a two-way process. On one hand, religion may justifiably be viewed as a powerful shaper of cultural traditions and social values. Conversely, there is equal utility in the proposition that religious ideas and practices are greatly influenced by the societies in which they are situated. In much of this book the former view has been adopted. Religious denominations and groupings of them have been treated as independent variables having face validity. Their roles in shaping patterns of regional culture and social pluralism have been thus far the primary focus of this study. However, in this chapter the alternate perspective is adopted. Having described and analysed religious trends and their consequences for patterns of both regionalism and pluralism in the 1952-1971 period, it must now be asked to what degree these religious trends may be attributed to more general social conditions? Can such social variables as population distribution and changes in it explain patterns of variance in these religious trends?

There is, of course, no contradiction in maintaining that patterns of religion are, at once, the causes of some social trends and the results of certain others. Social reality is a process in which any given social phenomenon may alternately be viewed as cause and effect. Having focused upon the social and cultural consequences of religious trends, we now ask, what has produced them in the first place? Such questions have historically been matters of dispute between social scientists and religionists. It is of little surprise that the latter often see religious trends as reflections of doctrine and belief. The former are apt to claim that religious phenomena are reflections of wider social mechanisms. In the broadest historical sense, the truth lies somewhere between this sociological reductionism and its antithesis, theological imperialism. The 1952-1971 *Archive of American Religious Denominations* provides an opportunity to empirically test both types of propositions.

From the outset of our work with these data and our initial plans to create the time-series *Archive of American Religious Denominations*, it was agreed that general social variables would be included in the *Archive*. The unique thing about the religious data in the 1952 NCCC and later 1971 studies is their county level of data collection. While United States Census studies are conducted at still smaller levels of geographic units, all such data are routinely aggregated to, and published at, the county level. Thus these two studies of religious adherence are the first of their type to be compatible with detailed population statistics. We noted in Chapter 2 that these religious data are in several ways equal, if not superior, to the quality of data contained in United States Census reports. The latter should be discussed here in some detail before using them in conjunction with the religious data.

A complete listing of those variables from the 1950 and 1970 *United States Census County and City Data Book*, that have been included in the *Archive of American Religious Denominations* are listed in Table 17. Two kinds of criteria have guided the selection of these particular variables. First, we have selected a series of fairly standard county level demographic measures, including population, migration, and dwelling unit statistics. A second cluster of measures are essentially socioeconomic status indicators, including degree of urbanization, and mean statistics for levels of education, income, and occupational categories. Lastly, a set of measures of economic activity, such as retail trade and manufacturing statistics are included. This diverse assortment of county level statistics, in both raw forms for 1950 and 1970, and as change rate data for the period, provides a rather comprehensive view of both demographic and socio-economic trends on a county by county basis for the 1950-1970 period. However, there are a number of problems relating to the use of these United States Census Bureau data.

A common problem encountered with general level measures such as county level statistics is the so-called ecological fallacy, that is, measuring things at one level and stating their implications at yet a different level of measurement. For instance, county level measures of income should not be equated with income statistics for the religious adherents in those counties; they are really two different things. A certain "leap of faith" is made in equating such different things. Such problems are compounded here because some of the raw county level data are also transformed by the Census Bureau into summary statistics such as mean and median indices. Moreover, as we noted at the outset of this study, there is some slippage in comparing religious data for 1952 and 1971 with socio-economic and demographic data for 1950 and 1970. Nonetheless, the utility of such complete sets of county level measures for both religious adherence and popula-

TABLE 17

County-level Demographic and Socio-economic Variables for 1950-1970 Included in the
Archive of American Religious Denominations

1950 VARIABLES	1970 VARIABLES
Population Rank 1950	Population Rank 1970
Total Population 1950	Total Population 1970
Population Increase 1940-50	Percent Change in Population 1960-1970
	Percent Net Migration 1960-1970
Percent Population Urban	Percent Urban
Percent Non-white	White Population
	Black Population
Median Age	Percent 18 yrs. and older
	Percent 65 yrs. and older
	Median Age
Median School Years	Median School Years Completed
Employed in Manufacturing	Percent Employed in Manufacturing
	Percent in Professions and Management
Employed in Agriculture	Total Farm Population
	Percent Change in Farm Population 1960-1970
Median Family Income	Median Family Income (All)
	Median Family Income (White)
	Per Capita Money Income
	Percent Families Below 125 percent of Poverty Level
Total Dwelling Units	Housing Units Year Round
	Percent Change in Housing Units 1960-1970
Owner Occupied Dwelling Units	Percent Owner Occupied Units
	Median Value of Owner Occupied Single Units
Retail Trade Sales (1954)	Total Retail Sales
Manufacturing Value Added (1954)	Manufacturing Value Added

NOTE: These measures are taken from the *United States Census County and City Data Books* for 1970 and 1950. The table is reprinted here from Halvorson and Newman (1978a) and is used with permission.

tion characteristics far outweighs these kinds of methodological problems. Compared to the complexities and often questionable sampling characteristics of many surveys, the flaws in these census and census-type data seem rather minor. In short, we place great confidence in them for examining basic aspects of the relationships between denominational religious patterns and general social conditions.

From the total list of population statistics included in the *Archive* and shown in Table 17, a somewhat shorter list of variables was selected for analysis here. These variables, shown in Table 18, were chosen according to two very different criteria. First, the selection of these variables was determined in part by the degree of comparability between measures used by the Census Bureau in 1950 and 1970. Over the past quarter century the Census Bureau has been involved in a gradual process of increasing the number of variables gathered and refining them as well. Accordingly, there are many more potentially useful county level variables for 1970 than for 1950 (see Table 17). Thus several variables in the *Archive* for 1970, and of potential interest here, are not available for time-series analysis for the 1950-1970 period. For instance, the 1970 variable for percentage of the county population 18 years of age and older would have allowed creation of an inverse statistic for the change rates in percentage of children in all counties. Such a measure would have been useful in directly testing Nash's idea (1968) that the religious revival was closely tied to the emergence of large numbers of school-aged children in the general population. However, that measure is not available in the 1950 *United States Census County and City Data Book*.

It should also be noted that between 1950 and 1970 the Census Bureau changed the so-called racial categories in which basic population statistics are collected. In 1950 a distinction between total population and non-white population is used. However, in 1970 the measurement categories are black and white, which together create total population. Obviously in the two time periods the residual category of non-black, non-white citizens are counted differently. As we noted earlier, because of the absence of black denominations in the religious data we have adjusted the total population statistics in the *Archive* to contain only white population, deleting non-whites in 1950 and blacks in 1970. Here again there is rather obvious and unfortunate slippage in the Census Bureau measures. These examples illustrate the ways in which the comparability of census variables between 1950 and 1970 imposed limits on our selection of variables for the following analysis.

The second major set of criteria guiding the selection of these variables were certain previously proposed hypotheses regarding the social elements that underlie adherence in religious organizations. For instance, we have already noted Nash's (1968) contention that increases in numbers of school-aged children in the population were a major factor causing the religious institutional growth during the years encompassed by these data. Median age statistics are a very crude measure of that variable. A well established body of literature argues that mainstream American religion is overwhelmingly middle class in composition (for a recent summary see Wilson 1978:288-307). Median school years and median income statistics are the best available county level measures for testing such a hypothesis. Sociologists and social geographers alike, including Zelinsky (1961), argue that urban—rural differences account for important variations in patterns of denominational religion. Accordingly, the variable for percent urban at the county level has been included. Obviously, the basic hypothesis that religious change reflects demographic change mandated an inclusion of such measures as county population sizes and sales and manufacturing indices. While again some of these measures at the county level seem to risk committing the ecological fallacy, they are the best census-based social indicators for the 1950-1970 period. These two criteria, comparability of measures and relevance to basic research hypothesis testing, determined the selection of the variables in Table 18.

TABLE 18

Selected County-level Demographic and Socio-economic Variables for 1950 and 1970

1950	1970
Total White Population	Total White Population
Percent Population Urban	Percent Urban
Median Age	Median Age
Median School Years	Median School Years Completed
Median Family Income	Median Family Income (White)
Total Dwelling Units	Housing Units Year Round
Retail Trade Sales	Total Retail Sales
Manufacturing Value Added	Manufacturing Value Added

While the socio-economic and demographic measures available clearly fall short of what might be required to test certain specific hypotheses, they surely are adequate for testing basic relationships between religious trends and general population trends. Given the level of generality in these measures (i.e., county level), we deemed it essential to examine their independence from one another as social indicators. In other words, it is important to ensure that these are not simply different ways of measuring the same aspects of general trends. In order to test this proposition we once again turned to the technique of factor analysis. It will be recalled that in Chapter 3 factor analysis techniques were used to identify those groupings of religious denominations that share common statistical, ethnic, theological, and regional associations. The same logic of the technique explains our use of it here. We wish to know if different socio-economic or demographic county level *measures* actually reflect the same or

different social variables. The results of this examination of the 1970 data are provided in Table 19. As before, SPSS library procedures were used (Nie 1975).

TABLE 19

A Factor Analysis of Selected Demographic and Socio-economic Measures for 1970

FACTOR	PERCENT OF VARIANCE EXPLAINED	CUMULATIVE PERCENT OF VARIANCE EXPLAINED	EIGEN VALUE FOR FACTORS
1	44.6	44.6	3.57
2	20.6	65.2	1.65
3	14.3	79.5	1.41
4	11.1	90.6	.88
5	6.1	96.7	.49
6	3.0	99.7	.24

FACTOR COMPOSITIONS		FACTOR LOADING
Factor 1:	Population	.982
	Dwelling Units	.986
	Manufacturing Value	.981
Factor 2:	Median Schooling	.953
	Median Income	.494
Factor 3:	Median Age	.990
Factor 4:	Retail Trade	.989
Factor 5:	Urbanization	.914
Factor 6:	Median Income	.801

The information in Table 19 provides important guidance for our interpretation of the relationships between these social indicators and the religious data. Clearly three of these items, those contained in Factor 1, are but different ways of measuring population size. County level population size, dwelling units, and value of manufacturing are alternate population size measures. As would be expected, these basic population indicators are the most powerful explanatory variables in the entire set. There is also a moderate association between median levels of schooling and median income, in Factor 2. These two commonly recognized measures of social class, schooling and income, taken together are the next most powerful explanatory variables. This makes a great deal of sense in terms of traditional social scientific analysis. Regardless of their theoretical perspectives, most social researchers agree that social class diferences are among the most powerful of all social indicators. Beyond Factors 1 and 2, the remaining items seem to maintain independent status, but as relatively weak socio-economic indicators. Having examined the relationships among these socio-economic and demographic variables, we may now examine their roles in determining patterns of denominational religion.

RELIGION AS A DEPENDENT VARIABLE

The late 1960s and early 1970s witnessed the emergence of a wide range of theories about the subjective causes of

TABLE 20

A Regression Analysis of Denominational Change for 1952-1971 and Population Change for 1950-1970

DENOMINATION	ALL COUNTIES r²	SIGNIFICANCE LEVEL	NEW COUNTIES r²	SIGNIFICANCE LEVEL
American Baptist U.S.A.	.091	.001	.004	*
American Lutheran	.317	.001	.061	.001
Baptist General Conference	.497	.001	.147	.001
Brethren in Christ	.045	*	.204	*
Catholic	.266	.001	.220	.001
Christian Reformed	.011	*	.319	.001
Church of the Brethren	.008	.001	.000	*
Church of God (Anderson)	.085	.001	.038	.01
Church of God (Cleveland)	.099	.001	.012	.01
Church of the Nazarene	.350	.001	.006	*
Cumberland Presbyterian	.007	*	.117	*
Episcopal	.208	.001	.763	.001
Evangelical Congregational	.030	*	.114	*
Evangelical Covenant	.256	.001	.007	*
Free Methodist	.185	.001	.050	*
Friends	.021	.001	.007	*
International Foursquare Gospel	.248	.001	.002	*
Jewish	.358	.001	.944	.001
Lutheran Church in America	.195	.001	.322	.001
Lutheran-Missouri Synod	.495	.001	.496	.001
Mennonite	.003	*	.225	*
Moravian—North and South	.031	*	.652	.001
Mormons (West only)	.056	.001	.000	*
N. A. Baptist General Conference	.117	.001	.080	*
Pentecostal Holiness	.015	.001	.015	*
Presbyterian U.S.	.459	.001	.265	.001
Reformed	.073	.001	.021	*
Southern Baptist	.159	.001	.000	*
Seventh Day Adventist	.068	*	.142	.001
Seventh-Day Baptist	.185	.001	.008	*
Unitarian Universalist	.003	*	.421	.001
UCC/Congregational	.166	.001	.070	.01
United Methodist/Evan. N.A.	.253	.001	.397	.001
United Presbyterian U.S.A.	.466	.001	.131	.001
Wisconsin Evan. Lutheran	.016	.01	.283	.001
All Denominations	.622	.001		

NOTE: * = not significant at the .01 level.

religious growth trends. Not only Kelley (1972) but other writers such as Berger (1967, 1969) and Greeley (1972b), to mention but a few, offer a wide assortment of ideological and social psychological explanations for why Churches alternately were expected to be either growing or shrinking, depending, of course, upon the brands of religion examined and the particular historic period scrutinized. From its inception our own work has aimed at a much simpler and more fundamental demographic hunch about the nature of religious organizational trends. Simply stated, we felt there was good reason to expect that basic population sizes and population change rates could explain much, and that geographic areas experiencing strong population increases would similarly experience increases in denominational religion. Similarly, we hypothesized that in instances where simple population sizes or population change rates were not sufficient explanatory variables, other socio-economic variables might emerge as significant; that such things as social class indicators, age characteristics, or urbanization might in one way or anoth-

er provide support for other socio-economic theories of religious organizational change. Accordingly, in this chapter we shall first look at the simple relationships between population change and denominational change. This will provide a direct statistical test of the basic hypothesis, previously suggested in several different ways by these data, that religious change is a function of population change. We shall next examine the more complex relationships emerging when the entire set of demographic and socio-economic indicators are entered into the analysis of both religious change and end-state religious patterns in 1971.

The technique used here is regression analysis. All regression techniques provide summary expressions of the relationships between two or more variables. In the first instance we have focused upon a single pair of dependent and independent variables, population and denominational figures. In the case of multiple regression techniques, the simultaneous effects of multiple independent variables upon a single dependent variable may be determined.

Both simple regression and multiple stepwise regression analyses are presented in this chapter. Religious adherence statistics for denominations at the county level in 1952 and 1971, and changes in them, are the dependent variables we seek to explain. County population sizes in 1950 and 1970 and changes in them, and subsequently the entire set of demographic and socio-economic indicators for these years serve as the independent variables. The statistic reported, r^2, ranges in value from 0 to 1. It reports the amount of variance in the dependent variable that is explained by the independent variable or variables. This is one of the most basic and frequently used statistics in all social science analysis (Nie 1975).

Table 20 provides a test of the simple hypothesis that changes in religious adherence at the denominational level between 1952 and 1971 were primarily a reflection of population changes, as measured here for the 1970-1950 period. Two different kinds of change data are examined. The left column of Table 20 provides r^2 statistics for all denominations in all counties in which each was located in either 1952 or 1971. A slightly different hypothesis is tested in the right hand column. Here only counties that have been newly penetrated by a particular denomination between 1952 and 1971 are included in the analysis. This essentially tests the strength of the three-variable relationship between religious growth, population growth, and geographic expansion by denominations.

The aggregate pattern, that is, the r^2 between change in adherence in all denominations and population change is by any standard quite high (.622) and is, moreover, higher than any of the denominational level figures. However, while it would be gratifying to claim that roughly 62 percent of the variance in all religious adherence for the period has been explained by this, we hesitate to do so. The two measures correlated here are so much alike that there is undeniable autocorrelation in this statistic. Stated differently, religious affiliation is a pervasive feature of voluntary joining in the United States. For the period in question more than 60 percent of Americans, as reported by any number of surveys and polls including the 1957 Census Bureau survey (1958), claimed some form of religious identity or adherence. These 1952-1971 data, account for over 50 percent of the entire United States population in both time periods. Obviously, the larger the proportion of the total population contained in any large subpopulation (such as all religious adherents) the more likely that a pervasive and normally distributed population characteristic will be correlated with population size and increases in it. For this same reason we found earlier in this chapter that the number of housing units in a county is a surrogate measure for the number of persons in that county (Table 19). This is also the reason why critics have justifiably claimed that Nash's (1968) comparison of yearly, national church membership figures and yearly statistics for numbers of school-aged children involve autocorrelation. We agree with those critics and maintain that changes in total religious adherence in

counties is most probably a surrogate measure for changes in population sizes in those counties. However, changes in denominational adherence are quite another matter.

In the United States denominational adherence to any particular religious group is not a surrogate measure of population and population change. There are manifold indications of the distinct realities of population and denominational religion. Religious groups vary greatly from one another in size, even when they occupy the same counties. As was seen in Table 5, while population during this period became rather more spatially concentrated, religious denominations exhibit no uniform change pattern in their degree of concentration. Additionally, religious groups remained substantially more concentrated than the general United States population over the period. In fact, the directionality of change in this index was different for the United States population than for many of the larger denominations. It is thus clear that individual religious denominations are not substitute measures for the total populations of the counties in which they are located. Rather, denominational patterns are distinct social variables, whose relationships to population change are a scientifically legitimate and empirically open issue. Table 20 brings substantial closure to that issue.

As the left hand columns in Table 20 indicate, while the specific strength of this relationship varies by denomination (ranging from nearly 50 percent to almost no variance explained), population change explains an impressive percent of the variance in most religious denominations. Interestingly, only eight of the 35 statistics reported here fail to reach statistical significance. These eight tend to represent smaller denominations that also have relatively small geographic coverage (see Table 4); only the Seventh Day Adventists vary from that pattern. It is also interesting that these eight denominations are found predominately in rural areas throughout the nation. However, one should not jump to conclusions about such underlying elements in these relationships.

It is true that statistical significance is more easily attained with large than with small samples or subpopulations. One might be led to claim that the size of most religious denominations guarantees statistical significance for these findings, and also determines the strength of the relationships (r^2) between these religious and population change variables. However, a close inspection of the left hand column in Table 20 refutes such claims. For instance, the largest denomination, Catholics, exhibits only moderate (.266) association with population change. Several large Protestant groups, including the United Presbyterians and the Missouri Lutherans, exhibit powerful r^2 statistics (.466 and .495). Yet other large denominations, including the Southern Baptists, the United Church of Christ, and the LCA Lutherans are not nearly so strongly related to population change (.159, .166, .195). Moreover, still other large denominations, prominently the American Baptist Churches, report a very low relationship to population change (.091). Thus, while it is possible that the overall sizes of most denominations tend to create an overestimation of statistical significance levels for all the data here, there is absolutely no evidence to support claims that the relative size of a denomination is a direct analogue to its degree of relationship to population change. Similarly, any claim that the size of denominations in general creates an autocorrelation problem is completely unsupported.

Thus far it is clear that rates of change in religious denominations between 1952 and 1971 and population change rates between 1950 and 1970 are rather strongly related, and that these relationships also vary quite a bit. Clearly, the adherence size of a denomination does not play a major role in the strength of such relationships. There is some slight indication that denominational families or types do play some kind of role. Both major Presbyterian groups fall toward the high end of the scale (.466 and .459), while both major Baptist denominations register very low (.091 and .159). However, the major Lutheran groups seem well spread over the entire range of r^2 values (.196, .317, and .495). Thus, for the moment at least, any argument for the role of either denominational families or regional types is not easily supported. Similarly, the low r^2 value (.003) for the Unitarian Universalists, a highly urbanized denomination, refutes any claim that urban-rural differences underlie patterns of variation in r^2 in Table 20.

The right hand columns of the table allow inspection of the three way relationship between change in adherence, change in population size, and spatial expansion by denominations. The r^2 statistic is calculated only on the basis of those counties that represent new turf for each denomination between 1952 and 1971. In this case, 17 of the 35 statistics fail to attain statistical significance. In simple terms, for almost half of these denominations there is no meaningful relationship between population change and change in adherence in the subset of counties they entered for the first time between 1952 and 1971. This trend supports two earlier findings discussed in Chapter 2, where it was shown that rates of spatial and numerical growth are not consistently related for these denominations. It was also shown that religious denominations tend to grow most in places where they are already established. Thus it makes a great deal of sense that the connection between change in adherence and change in population should be weaker, not stronger, for most groups in those counties into which they have only recently penetrated. Perhaps the most dramatic illustration of these several, related growth characteristics is provided by the Southern Baptist Convention. That denomination experienced impressive geographic expansion and equally impressive numerical and change rate growth for the 1952-1971 period. For newly entered counties only, a statistic of less than one percent of the variance explained is reported, which also is outside the realm of statistical significance.

There are, of course, some alternate cases in the table, that is, denominations reversing the general pattern and exhibiting a strong dependence upon changing populations in new turf areas. Jews (.944), Episcopalians (.763), Unitarian Universalists (.421) and United Methodists (.397) all fit this counter-trend. Moreover, these four exceptions to the general pattern have already been explained to a large degree in our earlier *Atlas* (1978b) and elsewhere (Newman and Halvorson 1979). Jews, Episcopalians, Unitarian Universalists, and Methodists are all denominations exhibiting strong movements into new areas between 1952-1971. The first three of these did so by virtue of regional shifts toward metropolitan areas in the western half of the nation; thus the statistics reported here are quite understandable. The United Methodists represent a complex situation. They were already a denomination with national geographic coverage in 1952. As was noted in the *Atlas*, their expansion into new areas was especially pronounced in the Plains states, generally an area of population stability and decline for the 1952-1971 period. However, the statistic reported here suggests that the incursions made by this denomination may have been more selective than we previously thought, with growing population areas being a major element in the United Methodist change pattern.

Table 20 may be summarized as follows. The basic theoretical proposition that changes in population size at the county level are significant predictors of changing sizes of adherence in religious denominations is verified. For most denominations the overall r^2 statistics are impressively high and for most denominations these relationships attain statistical significance. However, there is as yet no discernable pattern among denominations. Moreover, it is rarely the case that the relationship is stronger for the new turf counties. Obviously a more detailed inspection of the relationship between religious adherence and socio-economic indicators is required.

Table 21 advances the analysis of these relationships. Rather than a simple regression between two variables, the table shows the results of a multiple stepwise regression. The latter allows inspection of the individual and cumulative effects of a set of related independent variables upon a single dependent variable. While this procedure has been performed for the 1952, 1971, and change data for all denominations, only the latter two are presented here. The logic for focusing upon this part of the data is quite simple. We have seen throughout this book that the 1952 and 1971 relative distributions of most denominations and of total religious affiliation are virtually the same. There is no need to make things more complex by having to compare 1952 and 1971 data. In short, since there is little difference between broadscale religious patterns in 1952 and 1971, it simplifies the analysis to focus on the more recent data.

Table 21 contains several different pieces of information, all of which point even more impressively to a social and demographic theory of religious change and religious distribution. The multiple regression statistic r^2 ranges in value from 0 to 1, and much like a percent, shows the amount of variance in a dependent variable that may be explained or predicted by either a single independent variable or a related set of them. As with the earlier table, the next column provides the results of statistical significance testing. The last column in the table provides yet additional information. The multiple stepwise regression was performed for the entire set of eight demographic and socio-economic variables. Routinely, for each denomination most of the explained variance is accounted for by one of the eight variables and nearly all of the variance was accounted for by the first three such variables in every instance. Accordingly, we have provided in the last column

TABLE 21

A Stepwise Multiple Regression Analysis of Denominational Adherence for 1971 and Selected Demographic and Socio-economic Variables for 1970

DENOMINATION	CUMU-LATIVE r^2	SIGNIF-ICANCE LEVEL	FIRST THREE VARIABLES
American Baptist U.S.A.	.778	.001	DUS
American Lutheran	.536	.001	VAI
Baptist General Conference	.750	.001	VPD
Brethren in Christ	.220	*	IVT
Catholic	.924	.001	PDA
Christian Reformed	.224	.01	VAU
Church of the Brethren	.256	.001	IST
Church of God (Anderson)	.493	.001	PIS
Church of God (Cleveland)	.404	.001	PUS
Church of the Nazarene	.705	.001	DVU
Cumberland Presbyterian	.362	.001	UAS
Episcopal	.854	.001	PID
Evangelical Congregational	.669	.001	VDU
Evangelical Covenant	.663	.01	SIU
Free Methodist	.576	.001	DIU
Friends	.404	.001	VIS
International Foursquare Gospel	.795	.001	DPV
Jewish	.804	.001	DPV
Lutheran Church in America	.561	.001	PDI
Lutheran-Missouri Synod	.773	.001	VID
Mennonite	.151	*	PUV
Moravian—North and South	.433	.001	PDV
Mormons (West only)	.179	.01	ISU
N. A. Baptist General Conference	.434	.001	PDV
Pentecostal Holiness	.222	.001	ATS
Presbyterian U.S.	.739	.001	PID
Reformed	.401	.001	VIS
Southern Baptist	.783	.001	DPA
Seventh Day Adventist	.286	*	ATV
Seventh-Day Baptist	.383	.001	PUI
Unitarian Universalist	.601	.001	PID
UCC/Congregational	.697	.001	PDV
United Methodist/Evan. N.A.	.777	.001	PUD
United Presbyterian U.S.A.	.783	.001	PID
Wisconsin Evan. Lutheran	.220	.001	IST

NOTE: Key for variable abbreviations: P = population size; D = dwelling units; V = value added by manufacturing; S = median years of schooling; I = median income; A = median age; T = value of retail sales trade; U = urbanization. All measures are for county level 1970 census data.

In order to determine the directionality of the relationships in this table simple r and beta statistics were examined. For 31 of the 35 denominations the single variable accounting for most of the explained variance exhibits a positive correlation. The exceptions are: the Evangelical Covenant Church, the Mennonite Church, the Pentecostal Holiness Church, and the Seventh-Day Adventists. While negative relationships were occasionally found for other less powerful socioeconomic variables, these in no way modify the basic patterns already described.

* = not significant at the .01 level.

in Table 21 the letter abbreviations for the three most powerful variables for each denomination. The key for these abbreviations appears at the bottom of the table.

The first column in Table 21 is easily summarized. Correlations between all individual denominations and the eight population or socio-demographic variables in 1971 are high. Roughly one-third of the r^2 values (11 of 35) are over .5, meaning that over half of the variations in these denominational distribution patterns are explained by the eight population or socio-demographic variables at the country level. These values provide impressive support for a socio-demographic theory of religious adherence and change.

As would be required to support this theory, r^2 values are especially high for major denominations, among them Catholics, Jews, both Presbyterian groups, and United Methodists. Additionally, all but three r^2 values are reported as statistically significant. These three exceptions, the Brethren in Christ, the Moravians, and the Seventh Day Baptists, are among the smallest denominations, each appearing in 1971 in fewer than 100 counties (see Table 4). Similarly, the weakest statistically significant r^2 values are also for very small denominations with limited geographic distributions; among them are the Christian Reformed Church, the Evangelical Covenant Church, and the Mennonites (again, see Table 4). Thus, for the overwhelming majority of denominations, and certainly for all major denominations, the set of eight socio-demographic variables provide a powerful degree of explanation for patterns of religious adherence.

Lastly, the specific ordering of the socio-economic and demographic variables involved in these patterns of explained variance may be examined. It will be recalled that three of these variables, population size, dwelling units, and value added in manufacturing, are all sufficiently related to be viewed as alternate measures of population size (Table 19). As seen in Table 21, these three alternate measures substitute for one another in 26 of the 34 cases. In fact, only a few smaller denominations fail entirely to list one or another of these three population variables. Additionally, among these eight denominations, six do not list any of the three basic population surrogates. These trends prompt two general conclusions. First, substantial support is provided in Table 21 for the patterns first discovered in Table 20. Socio-demographic variables provide impressive levels of explained variance in denominational religion, and population size indicators at the county level are by far the most powerful such variables. A demographic theory of denominational patterns is strongly supported. Second and conversely, the particular measures available here offer much less support for alternative social explanations. Variables for degree of urbanization, age characteristics, and generalized social class measures such as years of schooling and income levels, play subordinate roles in these patterns.

While the relationship of denominational and population distribution as portrayed in Table 21 provides certain insights, the real thrust of our work with these data has been to explain the dynamics of change in the patterns of American religion. Consequently, Table 22 is of major significance because it involves the results of a multiple stepwise regression for changes in denominational statistics and changes in the entire set of eight demographic and socio-economic variables. As is the case with the 1971 religious data just discussed, the results are both highly variable and quite powerful in a statistical sense. It has been noted several times that the change rate measures used in this study are somewhat more difficult to interpret than absolute numerical data. Generally, the change data seem to yield less pronounced patterns than the 1952 or 1971 statistics. In this regard Table 22 is typical. The general level of statistical relationship is somewhat lower than that displayed in Table 21. However, Table 22 is also atypical for several reasons.

First, only five denominations failed entirely to attain an acceptable level of statistical significance for the relationships between denominational changes and changes in these eight social indicators. Those five include the Christian Reformed Church, the Evangelical Congregational Church, the Moravians, the Seventh-Day Baptists, and the Unitarian Universalists. With the exception of the last group, these denominations are all quite small and are generally associated with less urban areas. This group of denominations is similar to those failing to attain statistical significance in Table 21; none of them are major national denominations. Those denominations attaining relatively low statistical significance, the Brethren in Christ, the Cumberland Presbyterians, and the Mennonites, are also relatively small and concentrated in rural areas. While the last two such groups are fairly extensive in their distribution, all three are distinctly non-urban. Consequently, when viewed from the perspective of groups that fail to report statistically significant relationships between their changes in adherents and changes in the socio-economic indicators, such groups are clearly of secondary importance to broad national religious patterns.

Second, the levels of statistical significance are still quite strong overall, although somewhat less pronounced than those in Table 21. All of the major denominational groups attain statistical significance and most of these also fall among groups with the highest cumulative r^2 values. Although the values are slightly lower than those of the previous table, they are consistently strong.

Finally, the configuration of explanatory variables in the regression procedure is again quite revealing. The first, and therefore most powerful variable is drawn from one or another of the population surrogates in 23 of the 35 cases. Retail trade, which, as a change statistic rather than an end state (1970) statistic, is closely related to the population cluster, appears as a significant but distant second for six additional denominations. If these six denominations (Catholic, Church of God Anderson, Church of God Cleveland, Evangelical Covenant Church, Foursquare

TABLE 22

A Stepwise Multiple Regression Analysis of Changes in Denominational Adherence for 1952-1971 and Changes in Selected Demographic and Socio-economic Variables for 1950-1970

DENOMINATION	CUMU-LATIVE r^2	SINGIF-ICANCE LEVEL	FIRST THREE VARIABLES
American Baptist U.S.A.	.195	.001	PDT
American Lutheran	.356	.001	PAI
Baptist General Conference	.547	.001	PAV
Brethren in Christ	.111	.01	PVI
Catholic	.562	.001	TDV
Christian Reformed	.029	*	API
Church of the Brethren	.038	.001	VPD
Church of God (Anderson)	.192	.001	TIV
Church of God (Cleveland)	.220	.001	TSP
Church of the Nazarene	.449	.001	DAI
Cumberland Presbyterian	.024	.01	IVP
Episcopal	.330	.001	PDT
Evangelical Congregational	.353	.001	TIV
Evangelical Covenant	.128	*	IVT
Free Methodist	.255	.001	DSI
Friends	.030	.001	PIU
International Foursquare Gospel	.393	.001	TVI
Jewish	.400	.001	PDU
Lutheran Church in America . . .	.263	.001	PDT
Lutheran-Missouri Synod	.509	.001	PDA
Mennonite	.040	*	PSI
Moravian—North and South . . .	.069	.001	PSD
Mormons (West only)	.023	.01	IVT
N. A. Baptist General Conference	.180	.001	PDU
Pentecostal Holiness	.033	.001	PVT
Presbyterian U.S.	.488	.001	DSI
Reformed	.220	.001	TDS
Southern Baptist	.239	.001	DPI
Seventh Day Adventist	.105	*	PSV
Seventh-Day Baptist	.258	.001	DTS
Unitarian Universalist	.008	*	UIP
UCC/Congregational	.185	.001	PDI
United Methodist/Evan. N.A. . .	.260	.001	PTI
United Presbyterian U.S.A.	.460	.001	PDI
Wisconsin Evan. Lutheran	.064	.001	ATI

NOTE: Key for variable abbreviations: P = population size; D = dwelling units; V = value added by manufacturing; S = median years of schooling; I = median income; A = median age; T = value of retail sales trade; U = urbanization. All measures are for county level 1970 census data.

In order to determine the directionality of the relationships in this table simple r and beta statistics were examined. For 31 of the 35 denominations the single variable accounting for most of the explained variance exhibits a positive correlation. The exceptions are: the Christian Reformed Church, the Cumberland Presbyterian Church, the Evangelical Covenant Church, the Friends, the International Foursquare Gospel Church, and the Mormons. While negative relationships were occasionally found for other less powerful socioeconomic variables, these in no way modify the basic patterns already described.

* = not significant at the .01 level.

Gospel, and Reformed Church) are added to the 23 denominations already viewed as falling within the population cluster, only six relatively small denominations remain. The meaning of the connections of the Wisconsin Lutherans and the Christian Reformed group to changes in median age, or of the Evangelical Congregationalists, the Cumberland Presbyterians and the Mormons to changes in income, is not particularly clear. Of the remaining denominations, only the Unitarian Universalists display a pattern that is easily interpretable. That group, being distinctly urban in its distribution, is statistically tied to changes in the urban variable. However, this is one of the groups failing to attain statistical significance. For all the other groups, one or another of the population change surrogates emerges as the most powerful explanatory variable. We had anticipated that the basic population or demographic measures might emerge in many cases. The fact that these population surrogates so dominate the picture provides impressive support for a demographic theory of religious adherence and changes in religious adherence. Conversely, the strength of these findings also diminishes the plausibility of alternative theories, especially those focusing upon subjective types of variables.

While the consistently high values of r^2 statistics provide a felicitous theoretical outcome, one important gap in that theory remains. There is no apparent pattern to the variations in the strength of these statistics from one denomination to the next. In other words, we are unable to explain *why* some denominations are more strongly tied to population variables than others. While we have not provided the resulting tables here, several different ways of sorting the denominations fail to provide increased understanding of this problem. For example, neither the typology of regional groupings developed in Chapters 3 and 4 nor a simple aggregation by denominational family was useful in solving this problem. It is important that we attempt to resolve this one unexplained pattern in these data.

The somewhat disappointing performance of the remaining socio-economic variables, such as urbanism, median income, and median years of schooling, in contributing to patterns of explained variance may provide an important clue to these puzzling variations in r^2 values. It had been expected that these socio-economic variables would supplement the influences of the basic demographic variables. For instance, denominations that exhibit only moderate relationship to population size might otherwise be related to specific population features such as social class (income statistics) in a powerful way. Conversely, these socio-economic variables might have provided a gross additive effect to all denominations equally. But obviously neither of these things happened. There are at least two alternative explanations of these findings.

It could be argued that religious denominations, varying so greatly in size, locational features, and historical careers in the United States, are simply too diverse to admit to this degree of social explanation. However, the patterns of regional, ethnic, theological, and historical continuity exhibited by these data prevent us from accepting that view. For that matter, both the levels of statistical significance and the consistently high values of r^2 for most denominations in relation to the basic demographic variables point away from this interpretation. We remain convinced that there really should be clear patterns of r^2 values for different types of denominations.

The second explanation is that perhaps we have failed to measure accurately the variables that would produce such patterns. For example, in several places in this chapter we suggested that urbanization or its opposite, rural location, might provide explanations for otherwise elusive trends in the data. However, the county level measure of urbanization, or more precisely the degree of urbanization in counties, provided by the Census Bureau is not very useful in validating such explanations. The Census Bureau defines as urban an incorporated place having a population of 2,500. The county level measure calculates the percent of a county's total population that is living in such places. This method of calculation creates some very unfortunate results. For instance, a county containing a few relatively small communities but otherwise devoid of population would be classified as highly urban. Yet a highly populous county, in which a large proportion of residents live outside of the incorporated areas, would be designated as less urban. In actual practice, the use of this definition in the 1970 Census classifies the states of Utah, Nevada, and Arizona as more highly urbanized than Connecticut. Obviously this Census Bureau measure bears little empirical relationship to either our common sense information about such places or to more complex theories about processes of urban development and change. It seems fair to conclude that this measure is meaningless as a useful device with which to test such hypotheses.

Like Zelinsky (1961), we too have a strong hunch not only that religious denominations differ from one another on a broad geographic scale (regionalism), but also that types of localities (urban-rural differences) are involved in the relationships between religious adherence and socio-economic and demographic trends. Unfortunately this hypothesis extends beyond the capabilities of the measures in these United States Census Bureau data. Yet, if by "urban" one means cities larger than the census criterion of 2,500 persons, and frequently means metropolitan areas containing 50,000 or more persons, then our findings already suggest some support for the urbanism hypothesis. Obviously, the cluster of basic population or demographic variables that are so powerfully related to denominational adherence and change are also surrogate measures of what is commonly meant by urbanism (as opposed to the Census Bureau's definition). In this sense, support for the urban hypothesis is not so much missing from these data as hidden within them.

Similarly, these data also provide support for Nash's (1968) claim that changing age characteristics of the general population explain, in part, the religious revival. We had, of course, hoped to provide a more precise test of Nash's idea that school-aged children were a strong causal element in the return to institutional religion. However, county level aggregations of age group data to median age statistics are not really suitable for such an analysis. But the strength of county population sizes and changes, in explaining denominational adherence certainly provide empirical and theoretical support for Nash's theory. Denominations grow where populations grow, and surely biological reproduction and the maturing of children are a basic component in the general process of population expansion. The historical period under study experienced what has been labeled a "baby boom" or a population explosion; during the 1950-1970 period the United States population grew at a 35 percent rate. Obviously, even in the absence of a subjective theological awakening, religious denominations could not help but benefit from this pervasive population trend. As the regression analyses presented earlier have shown, this is precisely what happened.

These problems of measurement extend to the indicators for social class (i.e., income and schooling median statistics). As we noted at the outset of this chapter, when measured at the county level these indices are most susceptible to the ecological fallacy. It is really not at all

surprising that the measures account for very little explained variance.

In summary, subsequent to reviewing the consequences of religious trends between 1952 and 1971 for patterns of both regionalism and pluralism in the United States, this chapter has attempted to determine the degree to which religious trends are themselves the products of broader population trends. While some problems of measurement have been encountered, a clear and undeniable relationship has emerged from multiple stepwise regression analyses. While the patterns for denominations are quite variable, most of the religious groups contained in this data set exhibit strong relationships with basic demographic trends. In this sense, this chapter has provided strong validation for a demographic theory of religious adherence and religious change.

7

Examining The Conventional Wisdom

THE ISSUES IN PERSPECTIVE

All fields of research and scholarship work toward attaining a unified body of knowledge about the subjects studied. In its most complex form this information emerges as a coherent body of scientific theory. In yet a simpler form these ideas about "the way things are" become the conventional wisdom of the field, things that any informed person "ought to know." The conventional wisdom is called just that becuse its verity is decided upon by convention, by a somewhat diffuse process of agreement among a large number of experts, scholars, or researchers. The conventional wisdom is that part of a scientific field gradually translated into the popular culture of the times. For instance, the idea that a religious revival occurred during the third quarter of this century is a well established part of the conventional wisdom about religion, and is something about which informed lay persons are likely to be aware.

Given the reliance of social scientists interested in religious trends upon sample surveys, the 1952 and 1971 census-type studies of American religion have special potential. Since these data provide a previously unavailable portrait of religious trends for the period, they also may serve as a yardstick against which to measure the accuracy of the conventional wisdom. In this chapter the basic findings of our work with these data are summarized, and are compared to the established conventional images about American religion. Finally, the implications of these findings are explored.

There is little question that a religious revival occurred, if by that term one means a uniquely high resurgence of religious joining. Additionally, this trend ran well ahead of the similarly impressive population growth rate for the

roughly 20 year period. Various theories have been offered by both sociologists and theologians to explain this religious institutional growth pattern. These census-type data clearly indicate strong ties between denominational trends and population trends at the county level. It is hardly surprising to find this relationship for aggregate religious statistics. As we suggested in Chapter 6, autocorrelation very likely assures that total religious adherence will reflect total population, and that the two change indices will also be similarly related. After all, religion is a pervasive feature of voluntary joining in the United States. However, the strength of these relationships at the denominational level is quite another thing. Religious denominations exist in such great diversity precisely because people claim important historical and ideological differences from one another. Yet, with few exceptions, even at the denominational level, there are powerful statistical relationships between religious adherence and total population, and between changes in these two phenomena.

These findings do not negate other theories of religious joining and growth. They do, however, provide a context in which such theories may be evaluated and interpreted. Unfortunately, county level population measures from the United States Census do not allow quite the degree of precision required for testing certain theories. The relative weakness of socio-economic variables such as increases in school-aged children, urban-rural differences, and measures of social class (i.e., income and schooling statistics) in explaining religious patterns has been discussed extensively in Chapter 6. It was noted that both county level measurement and related problems of definition in these Census Bureau measures prevent detailed testing of these related theoretical propositions. Consequently, we have opted to withhold judgment on the utility of these hypotheses and to stress the need for further research with more refined measurements. Thus, the importance of basic demographic and population variables, and a demographic theory of religious adherence and change, constitutes the central theme here.

Inevitably, such considerations lead to an evaluation of theological explanations of religious trends and especially the so-called Kelley hypothesis (1972). It is widely recognized today that a downtrend in religious adherence began emerging in the late 1960s, and became especially pronounced in the middle 1970s. Kelley and others argue that religious conservatism was a key element in this trend among the Protestant denominations. However, the patterns depicted in these census-type data suggest an alternative hypothesis.

Chapter 2 has shown that, to some degree, Kelley's particular focus upon percent statistics tends to distort some parts of the trends for this period. Smaller, conservative denominations report high percent changes on the basis of small absolute shifts because of the small numbers of adherents they initially possess. However, it is clear from more recent studies that a certain group of mainstream Protestant Churches have disproportionately suffered the adverse effects of membership decline in the 1970s. These are the several branches of Anglo-Protestantism concentrated in our Type 4 grouping. These denominations share certain important features besides "theological liberalism."

The groups included here are Congregationalism (now UCC), Episcopalianism, the American Baptist Churches, the United Presbyterians, and the Unitarian Universalists. In 1952 both the United Methodists and the LCA Lutherans were also included in the Protestant branch of this major grouping. Several common features of these Protestant denominations noted in Chapters 3 and 4 should be reiterated here. With the exception of the Lutherans, these are all branches of Anglo-Protestantism. All of them, including the Lutherans, are the earliest colonial period Atlantic Coast denominations. They are obviously the core denominations of WASP culture in the northeastern United States. At the same time this wing of American Protestantism most shares what Herberg (1955) and others have called the "transmuting pot" of America's "three religion pluralism." More than any other group of Protestant denominations, these branches of English Protestantism share social and cultural space with the densest concentrations of European immigrant Catholics and Jews. As suggested earlier, this particular constellation of Anglo-Protestants, European Catholics, and Jews, concentrated in the Northeast and especially in metropolitan areas, has a very distinctive cultural meaning. This particular regional cluster epitomizes the "triple melting pot" phenomenon, in which, according to both Kennedy (1944, 1952) and Herberg (1955), broad religious identities have come to replace more specific religio-ethnic (i.e., denominational) identities. In other words, in the intense intergroup competition that developed, new definitions of group membership replaced older denominational labels. Most scholars

agree, for instance, that in the face of intense anti-Semitism, ethnic differences among immigrant Jews diminished in salience; being Jewish became a new form of ethnic identity. It is suggested here that much the same process has transpired for northeastern Anglo-Protestants, with a resulting de-emphasis of older denominational allegiances.

It is understandable that the United Methodists, the LCA Lutherans, and the United Presbyterians would be somewhat less affected by these trends. These three denominations experienced the greatest geographic shift away from the Northeast due to organizational mergers during this period. Our basic hypothesis is that conservative theology is not the key factor in differential growth rates among major denominations. As Yinger noted during the period (1961), ethnic religions did, in fact, participate in the religious revival of the 1950s. His observation would most certainly apply to the continental Reformation Churches in the American Midwest. In fact, only the northeastern Anglo-Protestants would fail to exhibit organizational vitality once the religious revival was over. Simply stated, Kelley claims that conservatives are the exception in the mid-1970s because they alone continue to grow. Conversely, it is suggested here that only the northeastern Anglo-Protestants failed to experience continued organizational strength.

Several trends in these 1952-1971 data suggest that this particular grouping of Protestant denominations should have experienced both organizational and cultural "softening." These are the only major Protestant groups not mainly concentrated in the growing population areas. Areas such as the South and the "Sunbelt" contain viable denominational alternatives for persons changing their regions of residence. Anglo-Protestants moving to the South readily find different regional branches of their traditional denominational family, especially the Southern Baptist, Southern Presbyterian, and United Methodist Churches. Similarly in the "Sunbelt," denominational names change a bit, but Baptism, Methodism, and Presbyterianism continue to flourish. Thus there are very logical alternatives that would explain patterns of denominational switching by Anglo-Protestants leaving the Northeast. One final point about these trends should be made. The Anglo-Protestant denominations of the northeastern states are the only major branch of American religion that did not benefit from massive immigration, internal population shift, or broad scale theological movements in the last 100 or so years. Both the Second Great Awakening and the later Holiness Movement (Ahlstrom 1972) provided membership infusions for the southern and western denominational groupings. Obviously internal population shift has favored these groups as well. The second wave of the Great Migration was a major component in swelling continental Protestanism in the American Midwest. Again the older northeastern Anglo-Protestants can claim no such influences from recent historical processes that contribute to organizational vitality.

Another major finding of this study is the remarkable stability of geographic patterns of American religion for this period. This too contradicts conventional ideas about the period. After all, the nearly 20 year interval between 1952 and 1971 encompasses the rise of the "Sunbelt" and the emergence of the so-called "New South." The previous dominance of the northeastern states in terms of population growth and such economic indicators as manufacturing was sharply eroded during these years. While there was a religious revival, and the change measures score highly in the South and Southwest, the overall pattern of American religion in the aggregate simply did not change. Stated differently, in an era of dramatic population and assumed cultural change, the basic pattern of American religion remained fixed. This fact holds at both the aggregate level and, as was shown both here and in our earlier *Atlas*, for most individual denominations as well. What are the social meanings of this degree of stability?

The remarkably stable characteristics of American denominational patterns between 1952 and 1971 suggest a number of things about religious joining in the United States. It must, however, be stressed that the following comments, like our analysis of the Kelley thesis, are within the realm of interpretation not fact. These are precisely the kinds of issues that require additional survey—especially attitudinal—research. With that qualification in mind, let us consider the possible meanings of these patterns of stability in American denominationalism.

A first conjecture is that people are more likely to switch their religious affiliations when making a geographic move than to take their old religious affiliations with them. It has been seen that denominations grew by 1971 where they were already strong in 1952. If it is maintained that population shifts during this period were substantial enough to register on institutional religious statistics—and most demographers would support that claim—then denominational switching is one leading explanation of the failure of religious data to reflect these population shifts.

Another way to state this is to suggest that broad scale patterns of religious affiliation are more dramatically affected by rapid periods of immigration than by in-migration, i.e., gradual periods of internal population shift and adjustment. Few would argue against the idea that the Great Migration, the two unprecedented eras of immigration in the last century, left permanant changes on the maps of population and religious population in the United States. Similarly, the dramatic cultural movements known as the Second Great Awakening and the Holiness Movement created lasting imprints on the religio-cultural map of the United States. But our ability to still measure those imprints in 1971 suggests that the religious revival of the 1950s was not a cultural movement of that type or significance. Its consequences appear to be much more quantitative than qualitative. All but one of the denominations in the 1952 and 1971 studies benefited numerically from the religious revival of the 1950s, but the map of American denominationalism did not change. Contrary to the assertions of Hill (1967) and others, these data provide no

statistical evidence of growing religious pluralism in the American South. Contrary to the claims of Shortridge (1976, 1977), no faltering of the Bible Belt is evident. Instead the data reveal numerical denominational growth accompanying population growth, but relative stability between most denominations throughout the period.

Denominational switching as an accompaniment to geographic movement may be only part of the story. Another possibility is that switching has also meant internal theological changes for denominations. Obviously such changes do not get measured in census-type data. These studies simply count heads, they tell us nothing about what those people think or believe. However, if regionally established religious organizations benefit from in-migration, those new members might well account for value changes in their communities and congregations. It is suggested that this is a crucially important issue for future survey research, for if this is in fact what is happening the emergence of a "New South," for example, will never be measurable in religious adherence statistics. Simply stated, religious affiliation may no longer be a reliable measure of regional culture and values in the United States. Religious organizational forms might remain very stable while dramatic internal value changes occur unnoticed by the census taker. Again these census-type studies are of substantial value in clarifying issues that are the appropriate focus of attitudinal research.

Religious regionalism has been a major focus of this study. The conventional wisdom maintains that there are distinct regional patterns of denominational dominance in American religion. Although we have verified that proposition, the regional groupings depicted here by factor analysis techniques are rather different from the regional typologies of previous researchers. Moreover, these data do not conform to the traditionally established culture regions. There is, of course, one important exception to that statement. Like almost all previous approaches to either religious or cultural regionalism, this study has encountered a southern region. While the remaining three national groupings, midwestern, northeastern, and western, do not conform to established views of regionalism in America, they do exhibit remarkable ethnic, theological, and historical continuity. Why these four types of religious groupings do not fit with much of the previous literature on either cultural or religious regionalism is an intriguing question.

A first possibility is that this study has more accurately measured these than did previous researchers. As noted in Chapters 3 and 4, there are certain important similarities between the present approach and that of Shortridge (1976, 1977). To the extent that these two approaches are similar, it is indeed argued that the data processing techniques, and the existence in this research alone of actual time-series data, have produced a superior result. As far as Zelinsky's (1961, 1973) approach is concerned, it has already been argued that it totally fails to test the relevant hypotheses upon which any regional typology must be based. The particular denominational groupings proposed in the present study, make great sense in historic terms and therefore portray both ethnic and theological continuities.

Although it is not difficult to understand why our typology of religious regionalism is so different from previously proposed typologies, its divergence from established views of cultural regionalism has some very serious implications for social scientists and especially cultural geographers. To begin, it is possible that religious adherence is simply a very poor measure of cultural differentiation in the United States. The inadequacies of denominational labels as measures of ethnic culture have already been noted; but the difficulties referred to here go beyond that problem. We are here suggesting that cultural regionalism and religious regionalism simply are not correlated in the way that most students of either subject have previously assumed. If, however, one wishes to reject that claim, a more serious implication emerges. Perhaps religious and cultural regions do coincide, in which case the long established cultural regions (i.e., those of Zelinsky and others) are simply convenient scholarly fictions, or an outdated conventional wisdom. Resolving these issues is obviously beyond the scope of this study. However, it is inescapable that the statistical and interpretative strength of the religious regions depicted here raises some major issues for students of both religious and cultural regionalism in the United States. At the very least, a reconceptualization of the nature of religious regionalism and its relationship to cultural regionalism is in order.

RETROSPECTIVE THOUGHTS

Our work with the 1952 and 1971 *Churches and Church Membership in the United States* studies was motivated by the idea that these unique collections of data could provide new insights into and views of the American religious landscape. As we hope the foregoing chapters have demonstrated, these expectations were well founded. This book has been written from the combined perspective of the sociology of religion and social geography. Accordingly, the patterns created by these time-series data for 1952 and 1971 have challenged certain areas of the conventional wisdom of both fields in several different ways.

While throughout the study we have stressed the utility of census-type data, it should be clear that the connections between these kinds of data and both survey research and social theory are the areas where the greatest scientific advances are to be found. On the one hand, we are gratified that these census-type data have allowed very basic level theory testing. In this sense, context and perspective are created for additional theoretical avenues not directly testable with these kinds of statistics. On the other hand, while census-type data are weakest in addressing subjective issues, they point to important areas for future survey research. Statistical data never speak for themselves, and it must be reiterated that inference and conjecture have been unavoidable. Comprehensive data files have a way of raising as many issues as they resolve. There are various avenues for testing the accuracy of the more speculative issues we have raised here. The public availability of the *Archive of American Religious Denominations 1952-1971* assures that other researchers may re-examine the patterns depicted here and our analysis of them. Certain of our ideas are only directly testable by survey methods, and we surely hope that this volume generates such studies. Finally, the scheduled 1980 census-type study of religious denominations will provide an occasion for testing both our speculative assertions and the longevity of the objective trends depicted here and in the earlier *Atlas*.

Bibliography

Abramson, Harold J.
1973   *Ethnic Diversity in Catholic America.* New York: John Wiley.

Ahlstrom, Sidney E.
1972   *A Religious History of the American People.* New Haven, Connecticut: Yale University Press.

American Jewish Committee
1971   *American Jewish Yearbook*, vol. 72. New York: American Jewish Committee.
1976   *American Jewish Yearbook*, vol. 77. New York: American Jewish Committee.

Bennion, Lowel
1976   Privately circulated manuscript containing data for the Church of Jesus Christ of Latter-Day Saints (Mormons) in the western United States for 1971.

Berger, Peter L.
1967   *The Sacred Canopy.* Garden City, New York: Doubleday.
1969   *A Rumor of Angels.* Garden City, New York: Doubleday.

Carroll, Jackson W., Douglas W. Johnson and Martin E. Marty
1978   *Religion in America: 1950-present.* New York: Harper & Row.

Fukuyama, Yoshio
1963   "The Uses of Sociology; by Religious Bodies," *Journal for the Scientific Study of Religion*, 2: 195-203.

Gaustad, Edwin S.
1962   *Historical Atlas of Religion in America.* New York: Harper & Row.

Glock, Charles, and Rodney Stark
1965   *Religion and Society in Tension.* Chicago: Rand McNally.

Goldstein, Sidney
1969   "Socioeconomic Differentials among Religious Groups in the United States," *American Journal of Sociology*, 74: 612-631.

Greeley, Andrew
1972a   *The Denominational Society.* Glenview, Illinois: Scott, Foresman.
1972b   *Unsecular Man.* New York: Schocken.

Grupp, Fred W. Jr., and William M. Newman
1973   "Political Ideology and Religious Preference: The John Birch Society and the Americans for Democratic Action," *Journal for the Scientific Study of Religion*, 12: 401-13.

Halvorson, Peter L. and William M. Newman
1978a   "A Data Archive of American Religious Denominations, 1952-1971," *Review of Religious Research*, 20: 86-91.
1978b   *Atlas of Religious Change in America*, 1952-1971. Washington, D.C.: Glenmary Research Center.

Herberg, Will
1955   *Protestant-Catholic-Jew.* Garden City, New York: Doubleday.

Hill, Samuel S. Jr.
1967   *Southern Churches in Crisis.* New York: Holt, Rinehart & Winston.

Hudson, Winthrop
1953   *The Great Tradition of the American Churches.* New York: Harper & Row.

Irwin, Leonard G.
1976   *Supplemental Data for Churches and Church Membership in the United States 1971.* Atlanta, Georgia: Southern Baptist Home Mission Board.

Isard, W.
1960   *Methods of Regional Analysis.* Cambridge, Mass.: MIT Press.

Johnson, Douglas W., Paul Picard and Bernard Quinn
1974   *Churches and Church Membership in the United States 1971.* Washington, D.C.: Glenmary Research Center.

Jones, Maldwyn Allen
1960   *American Immigration.* University of Chicago Press.

Jordan, Terry G.
1969   "Population Origins in Texas, 1850," *Geographical Review*, 59: 83-103.

Kelley, Dean
1972   *Why Conservative Churches Are Growing.* New York: Harper & Row.

Kennedy, Ruby Jo Reeves
1944   "Single or Triple Melting Pot? Intermarriage Trends in New Haven, 1870-1940," *American Journal of Sociology*, 49: 331-339.
1952   "Single or Triple Melting Pot? Intermarriage Trends in New Haven, 1870-1950," *American Journal of Sociology*, 58: 56-59.

King, Morton and Richard Hunt
1967   "Measuring the Religious Variable: Nine Proposed Dimensions," *Journal for the Scientific Study of Religion*, 6: 173-190.
1972   *Measuring Religious Dimensions.* Dallas: Southern Methodist University Press.

Knoke, David
1974   "Religion, Stratification and Politics: America in the 1960s," *American Journal of Political Science*, 18: 331-345.

Littel, Franklin H.
1962   *From State Church to Pluralism.* Garden City, New York: Doubleday.

Marty, Martin
1958   *The New Shape of Religion in America.* New York: Harper & Row.

Mead, Sidney
1963   *The Lively Experiment.* New York: Harper & Row.

Mueller, Samuel and Angela Lane
  1972   "Tabulations Form of the 1957 Current Population Survey on Religion," *Journal for the Scientific Study of Religion*, 11: 76-98.

Nash, Dennison
  1968   "A Little Child Shall Lead Them: A Statistical Test of the Hypothesis that Children Were the Source of the American Religious Revival," *Journal for the Scientific Study of Religion*, 7: 238-340.

NCCC
  1953   *Yearbook of American Churches 1952*, ed. Benson Y. Landis. New York: National Council of the Churches of Christ.

  1972   *Yearbook of American and Canadian Churches 1971*, ed. Constant H. Jacquet Jr. New York: National Council of the Churches of Christ.

Newman, William H.
  1973   *American Pluralism*. New York: Harper & Row.

Newman, William M., Peter L. Halvorson and Jennifer Brown
  1977   "Problems and Potential Uses of the 1952 and 1971 National Council of Churches' 'Churches and Church Membership in the United States' Studies," *Review of Religious Research*, 18: 167-173.

Newman, William M. and Peter L. Halvorson
  1979   "American Jews: Patterns of Geographic Distribution and Change, 1952-1971," *Journal for the Scientific Study of Religion*, 18: 183-193.

Nie, H. L., *et. al.*
  1975   *SPSS: Statistical Package for the Social Sciences*, 2nd ed. New York: McGraw-Hill.

Niebuhr, H. Richard
  1929   *The Social Sources of Denominationalism*. New York: Henry Holt.

Petersen, William
  1962   "Religious statistics in the United States," *Journal for the Scientific Study of Religion*, 2: 165-178.

Rummel, R. J.
  1970   *Applied Factor Analysis*. Evanston, Illinois: Northwestern University Press.

Shannon, C. and W. Weaver
  1949   *The Mathematical Theory of Communications*. Urbana: University of Illinois Press.

Shortridge, James
  1976   "Patterns of Religion in the United States," *Geographical Review*, 66: 420-434.

  1977   "A New Regionalization of American Religion," *Journal for the Scientific Study of Religion*, 16: 143-153.

Sopher, David
  1967   *Geography of Religions*. Englewood Cliffs, N.J.: Prentice-Hall.

Swatos, William H. Jr.
  1976   "Weber or Troelstch? Methodology, Syndrome, and the Development of the Church-Sect Theory," *Journal for the Scientific Study of Religion*, 15: 129-144.

Stark, Rodney and Charles Y. Glock
  1968   *American Piety*. Berkeley: University of California Press.

U.S. Census Bureau
  1958   *Religion Reported by the Civilian Population of the United States, March 1957*, Series P-20, Number 79. Washington, D.C.: United States Department of Commerce, Bureau of the Census.

Whitman, Lauris and Glen Trimble
  1954   *Churches and Church Membership in the United States 1952*. New York: National Council of the Churches of Christ.

Wilson, John
  1978   *Religion in American Society*. Englewood Cliffs, N.J.: Prentice-Hall.

Yinger, J. Milton
  1961   *Sociology Looks at Religion*. New York: Macmillan.

Zelinsky, Wilbur
  1961   "An Approach to the Religious Geography of the United States: Patterns of Church Membership in 1952," *Annals of the American Association of Geographers*, 51: 139-193.

  1973   *The Cultural Geography of the United States*. Englewood Cliffs, N.J.: Prentice-Hall.

Index

NAMES

Abramson, Harold J., 36, 59
Ahlstrom, Sidney E., 56, 59

Bennion, Lowel, 6, 59
Berger, Peter L., 48, 59
Brown, Jennifer, 1, 60

Carroll, Jackson W., 2, 59

Fukuyama, Yoshio, 3, 59

Gaustad, Edwin S., 3, 59
Glock, Charles Y., 14, 17, 59
Goldstein, Sidney, 1, 59
Greeley, Andrew, 17, 36, 48, 59
Grupp, Fred W. Jr., 14,59

Halvorson, Peter L., 1, 5, 6, 12, 19, 22, 23, 28, 29, 32, 46, 50, 59, 60
Herberg, Will, 3, 7, 22, 29, 56, 59
Hill, Samuel, S. Jr., 21, 57, 59
Hudson, Winthrop, 7, 59
Hunt, Richard, 18, 59

Irwin, Leonard G., 6, 59
Isard, W., 10, 59

Jacquet, Constant H. Jr., 60
Johnson, Douglas W., 1, 2, 3, 59
Jones, Maldwyn Allen, 22, 59
Jordan, Terry G., 28, 59

Kelley, Dean, 7-8, 13, 48, 56, 57, 59
Kennedy, Ruby Jo Reeves, 29, 56, 59
King, Morton, 18, 59
Knoke, David, 14, 59

Landis, Benson Y., 60
Lane, Angela, 1, 60
Littel, Franklin H., 3, 14, 59

Marty, Martin, 2, 7, 59
Mead, Sidney, 7, 60
Mueller, Samuel, 1, 60

Nash, Dennison, 46-47, 49, 53-54, 60
Newman, William M., 1, 5, 6, 12, 14, 19, 22, 23, 28, 29, 32, 36, 46, 50, 59, 60
Nie, H. L., 19, 49, 60
Niebuhr, H. Richard, 14, 17, 60

Petersen, William, 1, 60
Picard, Paul, 1, 3, 60

Quinn, Bernard, 1, 3, 59

Rummel, R. J., 19, 25, 60

Shannon, C., 39, 60
Shortridge, James, 2, 15, 16-17, 18, 19-21, 23, 25, 30, 32-34, 35, 36, 39, 57, 60
Sopher, David, 2, 3, 15, 16, 17, 19-20, 23, 25, 60
Stark, Rodney, 14, 17, 60
Swatos, William H. Jr., 14, 60

Trimble, Glen, 1, 2-3, 60

Weaver, W., 39, 60
Whitman, Lauris, 1, 2-3, 60

Williams, Roger, 22
Wilson, John, 47, 60

Yinger, J. Milton, 56, 60

Zelinsky, Wilbur, 1, 3, 10, 15-16, 17, 19-20, 23, 25, 30, 32-34, 35, 36, 47, 53, 57-58, 60

SUBJECTS

American Baptist Churches in the U.S.A., 4, 8, 9, 18, 48, 51, 52, 56
   as a regional group, 21-22
   See also Baptists
American Evangelical Lutheran Church, 5
American Lutheran Church (ALC), 4, 5, 8, 9, 14, 18, 48, 51, 52
   as a regional group, 20, 22
   See also Lutherans
American Jews
   See Jews
Anglican Church, 20, 22
   See Episcopal Church
Anglo-Calvinists, as a regional type, 23, 28, 30, 32-34
Anglo-Protestants, as a regional type, 21-22, 23, 28, 30, 32-34
Archive of American Religious Denominations, 2-6, 45-47
Assemblies of God, 4
Augustana Evangelical Lutheran Church, 5

Baptist General Conference, 4, 6, 8, 9, 18, 48, 51, 52
   as a regional group, 20, 21
Baptists, as a family of denominations, 50
   as a regional group, 15, 16, 20-22, 23, 28, 30
   See also specific groups
Brethren in Christ, 4, 8, 9, 18, 48, 51, 52
   See also Brethren
Brethren, as a family of denominations, 36
   as a regional group, 23, 30

Calvinists, Dutch, as a regional type, 23-24, 30, 32-34
Catholic Church (Roman), 3, 4, 7, 8, 9, 10, 17, 18, 19, 48, 49, 51, 52, 56
   as a regional group, 15, 16, 20-22, 23, 29
   ethnic diversity within, 35-36
   special geographic features, 12, 30-31, 34
Christian Reformed Church, 4, 8, 9, 18, 48, 51, 52
   as a regional group, 23-24
Church growth
   causes of, 7-9, 13, 47-54, 55-57
   general trends in, 4-5, 7-13
   maps, 11-12
   theories about, 7-9, 46-47
Church of God (Anderson), 4, 8, 9, 12, 18, 48, 51, 52
   as a regional group, 21
Church of God (Cleveland), 4, 8, 9, 12, 18, 48, 51, 52
Church of the Brethren, 4, 7, 8, 9, 18, 48, 51, 52
   See also Brethren

Church of the Nazarene, 4, 8, 9, 18, 48, 51, 52
   as a regional group, 15, 21-22
   special geographic features, 30-31
Churches of Christ, 4
Cluster analysis, 16-17
Congregational Christian Churches, 4, 5, 8, 9, 18, 48, 51, 52
   See also United Church of Christ
Congregationalists
   See United Church of Christ *or* Congregational Christian Churches
Conservative Mennonite Conference, 5
Cumberland Presbyterian Church, 4, 8, 9, 18, 48, 51, 52
   See also Presbyterians

Disciples of Christ
   as a regional group, 15

Entropy index
   described, 39
   maps, 40, 42
   results from, 41-44
Episcopal Church (Protestant Episcopal Church), 4, 7, 8, 9, 14, 18, 48, 50, 51, 52, 56
   as a regional group, 15, 22, 30
Ethnic groups
   as different from denominational groups, 35-36
   within denominational groupings, 18-24
Evangelical and Reformed Churches, 5, 20, 22
   See also United Church of Christ
Evangelical Church of North America, 4, 5, 8, 9, 18, 48, 51, 52
   as a regional group, 20
Evangelical Congregational Church, 4, 8, 9, 18, 36, 48, 51, 52
   as a regional group, 23
Evangelical Covenant Church, 4, 8, 9, 18, 36, 48, 51, 52
   as a regional group, 23
Evangelical Lutheran Church, 5
Evangelical United Brethren, 5
   See also United Methodist Church

Factor analysis
   of religious denominations
      described, 18-19
      factor scores, 25
      maps, 26, 27
      results from, 19-24
   of social indicators, 47
Finnish Evangelical Lutheran Church, 5
Free Methodist Church, 4, 8, 9, 18, 48, 51, 52
   as a regional group, 21
   See also Methodists
Friends World Committee, 4, 5, 8, 9, 18, 48, 51, 52
   as a regional group, 15, 21

Hartford Seminary Foundation, 1
Holiness Methodist Church, 5

Immigration
   effects upon regionalism, 22, 29, 56-57
Index of concentration
   described, 9
   results from, 9-12